the PREACHER
and his work

College Lectures to
Student Preachers

revised and enlarged by
Jack Meyer, Sr.

1217 Crestwood Dr.
Cleburne, TX 76033
www.Azimuth.Media

Copyright © 2019 Azimuth Media

Paperback:
ISBN-13: 978-1-62080-153-6

eBook:
ISBN-13: 978-1-62080-254-0

Library of Congress Control Number: 2019930589
Version 1.0

All rights reserved. This book or parts thereof may not be reproduced in any form without written permission from the publisher.

**Discover Other Titles
By Azimuth Media
www.Azimuth.Media**

DEDICATION

To my faithful wife, who has stood by me, helped me, and shared with me the responsibilities, sacrifices, and ample compensations of a preacher's career; to our son, Jack, a Gospel preacher of twelve years' experience; and to our daughter, Joan, who has finished her first two years in a Christian college.

INTRODUCTION TO THE FIRST EDITION

While I was president of Florida Christian College, 1946-49, we tried to secure the services of Brother Jack Meyer in our Bible department. Unfortunately, for us, he was not in position to accept our invitation. Later, when I was head of Central Christian College, in Bartlesville, Oklahoma, another effort was made to obtain his services. He gave serious consideration to our offer, but once more felt compelled to decline.

On a number of occasions, Brother Meyer was invited to address the student body in the above mentioned colleges. At different times, he spoke at our chapel exercises, he appeared on our Annual Lectureships, and he rendered valuable service to our work in other ways. Brother Meyer is a true friend of Christian education. He did much to encourage us at Central Christian College. He has always encouraged parents to send their children to Christian schools and to give of their means to such works. Brother Meyer loves people; he also loves the Word of God, and he is unwilling to sacrifice truth for the sake of any individual.

In February of 1953, we had Brother Meyer for a week of intensive work at Central Christian College. He delivered a number of lectures each day. Some of these were to the entire student body, but most of them were directed primarily toward those who were planning to become preachers, teachers, or wives of preachers and teachers. These lessons were intended to be practical and helpful in meeting the everyday problems that Christian workers inevitably encounter. Many of the suggestions grew out of actual experiences. Brother Meyer had all of his lessons well outlined and mimeographed when he presented them—as he always does. All who heard them agreed that they should be published, so that others might have the benefit of them. I am glad that he has seen fit to acquiesce in these suggestions.

It is both a privilege and a pleasure to me to commend this work. I hope that many of our preachers, especially our younger preachers, will study these lessons thoroughly. They will profit much by doing so.

L. R. Wilson
Central Church of Christ
Amarillo, Texas

ENCOURAGEMENT FOR THE PREACHER

In this age when the number of congregations is increasing at a greater rate than the number of Gospel preachers, it is encouraging for me to see this revised and enlarged edition of the book, The Preacher and His Work, by Jack Meyer, Sr.

In November of 1954, Brother Meyer came to David Lipscomb College and delivered an excellent series of lessons on the general theme, "College Lectures to Student Preachers." The fruit of this series is still being seen in the lives of the young men who had the course. Brother Meyer was at his best in the delivery of these lectures.

Jack Meyer, Sr. has always been known as one who is firm in his convictions and who is willing to stand for the same. His interest in young preachers has made it possible for a number of young men to be preaching now who would not have been able to do so otherwise. This book is a continuation of such interest. The ones who read it can become better preachers as a result of these lessons.

Willard Collins

AUTHOR'S PREFACE TO THE FIRST EDITION

The author of this book was invited by Brother L. R. Wilson, then president of Central Christian College, Bartlesville, Oklahoma, to deliver a series of thirteen lectures to the student preachers of that college, February 2-6, 1953. The object of this special course of study was to lay before the young men the work of the Gospel preacher, with particular reference to those men who are employed by congregations to spend the major portion of their time with said churches. The lectures dealt almost not at all with points of controversy—though the speaker shunned no question on any point of dispute, and he urged the young preachers to make their stand on all questions as clear as crystal. But we were majoring on the day-by-day mechanics of the work of preaching and details of developing a congregation as a scripturally working force. In addition to three classes on each of four days, and one class on the night of the opening day, there was a chapel speech each day on the subject of "The New Testament Church."

David Lipscomb College, Nashville, Tennessee, through its vice president, Brother Willard Collins, invited the author to present the same course of study to the student preachers of that institution, November 1-4, 1954, in a series of six lectures. Four full class-length speeches in the same field of study were added, through the invitations of the teachers of as many classes.

The author does not claim to be an authority on the subject of preaching and building a congregation. But the colleges brought me to their campuses for the assigned task, and I did the best I could to present what little I know about the best work in which a man may engage in this life.

The following chapters cover the ground of those lectures, as originally presented. The chapters are differently arranged in some places, to be better adapted to a book. But the material of the book is practically the same as given in the two colleges, with only slight variation—and that only in the interest of strengthening the course of study. From the conclusion of the first series of lectures until the present, there has been a steady demand that the material be put into book form. Brother B. C. Goodpasture, editor of The Gospel Advocate, Nashville, Tennessee, asked for "twelve or fifteen" articles covering the matter presented. Consequently, fourteen articles were written and published in that journal from June through October, 1953. I am grateful to the two schools and the paper for thus using this material, and it is finally presented in this form, with a fervent prayer that our God may bless it to the prospering of the Gospel of Christ.

Jack Meyer, Sr. (May 16, 1955)

PREFACE TO REVISED AND ENLARGED EDITION

Under the blessings of our God and the kindness of a responsive public, the first edition of The Preacher and His Work was sold out in slightly over two years. Brethren in general, and preachers in particular, have urged that the work not be allowed to cease being in print, and that even a larger edition be published. This interest has been so widespread, uniform, and insistent, that we could not in good conscience avoid publishing the present work.

The owner of the copyright of the first edition generously allowed the author to quote at will from that production, for which goodness profound gratitude is here expressed. Large sections of this volume are identical with the first one, but scattered all through this edition are many revisions and additions. While this edition will substantially reproduce the lectures as first given to the student preachers of Central Christian College, now of Oklahoma City, OK, and David Lipscomb College, Nashville, TN, as well as the long series of articles appearing in The Gospel Advocate, Nashville, TN, no effort has been made here to confine the material to that of those lectures and articles. On the contrary, our purpose here has been to use said lectures and articles as a base, but making revisions and enlargements which will add usefulness to the book; this is especially true in certain sections which were judged to be too brief in the first edition, and in other places keeping in mind certain developments of the past three years. Particular attention is called to a difference in this volume on the point of the rights of congregations to support orphan homes which are not under the oversight of congregational elders, as opposed to the view set forth in the first edition, page 140, that it is safe for them to be under the oversight of congregations. This new work is truly a "Revised and Enlarged Edition."

The author's boundless gratitude is here expressed to so many who made possible the quick exhausting of the supply of the first edition. It is my hope that the material of this new edition may be received with even more favor and enthusiasm, and that readers will work to place it in the hands of preachers, church leaders, and members in general. This edition deals not only with the mechanics of preaching and building congregations, in which all Christians should be interested, but gives attention also to some of the controversial battlefields on which Christian soldiers must fight, and more so than in the original lectures.

Again, I express "a fervent prayer that our God may bless it to the prospering of the Gospel of Christ."

            Jack Meyer, Sr. (February, 1960)

TABLE OF CONTENTS

IN THE CONGREGATION 1

THE PREACHER'S FAMILY 11

THE PREACHER'S LIBRARY 21

STUDY AND RELATED MATTERS 35

RECREATION AND RELATED MATTERS 49

SPECIAL PITFALLS (PART 1) 9

SPECIAL PITFALLS (PART 2) 69

SPECIAL PITFALLS (PART 3) 79

SPECIAL PITFALLS (PART 4) 95

THE PROBLEM OF VISITING 109

DEVELOPING THE CHURCH IN WORK (PART 1) 119

DEVELOPING THE CHURCH IN WORK (PART 2) 137

DEVELOPING THE CHURCH IN WORK (PART 3) 147

TRENDS AND CRITICAL BACKGROUNDS 171

OPPORTUNISTS AND DISCOURAGEMENTS 201

CHAPTER 1
THE PLACE OF THE PREACHER IN THE CONGREGATION

A majority of young preachers go from college into congregations as full-time, paid evangelists, spending most of their time in said communities. Some obtain secular employment and also preach for congregations which cannot at first afford full-time preachers. Still others give full time to protracted meetings. But that third class usually does that later in life, first going through either of the two preceding stages. Either class, however, labors in a congregation for a season. Hence, in whatever capacity the preacher serves a church, it logically challenges our attention first in this series to raise the question: "What is the place of the employed preacher in a congregation?"

I. **Does a church have the scriptural right to employ a full-time preacher, working with and through that church for a major part of his time?**
   A. In support of an affirmative answer to this question, I submit five points:
      1. There is the New Testament law that the Gospel supports the preacher. (1 Cor. 9:14)
      2. There is the New Testament law that the church supports the truth. (1 Tim. 3:15)
      3. There is the New Testament law that the congregation is an independent, self-governing body, through its elders as overseers. (Acts 20:28)
      4. Therefore, the church necessarily has the right to support preachers of the Gospel anywhere, where

not in violation of other New Testament law.
  5. Preachers of the Gospel thus have the right to accept such offer of support anywhere.
B. But, you will encounter these objections, which must be fairly considered and scripturally settled:
  1. "There is no New Testament example of a preacher being employed by a church to work with it, in its home locality, for several years." We reply, there is no New Testament law as to how long a preacher shall stay at one place. As to the length of a preacher's stay with a congregation, there are varied examples in the New Testament. Paul was at Ephesus for at least two years. (Acts 19:10) He was at Corinth at least one and one-half years. (Acts 18:11) Acts 13:1 records a plurality of "prophets and teachers," Paul among the number, at Antioch even at one time. How long they remained, how they divided and apportioned their work, is not revealed. Since the time of the stay varied, and is not specified as to uniform length, that point is left to the judgment of the church, and we have no right to make a law.
  2. "As generally practiced today, the preacher takes charge." This I deny. Gospel preachers are universally stressing that the bishops, or elders, are the overseers and in charge of the churches. When you enter upon a work with a church, make it clear that such is your attitude. Now, one elder may have an influence excelling that of the other elders. In practically all congregations, one elder stands out above the others in influence. Again, sometimes we hear of one elder stepping out of bounds and "lording it over" all others. But that does not prove all elders are dictators, nor does it argue for abolishing the eldership. In like manner, a preacher may have such an influence or so act, but without that proving that "the preachers are taking charge of the churches."
  3. "Elders should feed the flock and let the preachers preach elsewhere." One of the common mistakes made by those who object to a church being preached to and otherwise served by a full-time preacher can be found in the Wallace-Ketcherside Debate, 1952, where W. Carl Ketcherside, of St. Louis, says, "You cannot preach the Gospel to the church..."

(pg. 22) On page 23, he quotes from Leroy Garrett, in Jas. A. Allen's paper, The Apostolic Times, saying, "There is no record of anyone preaching to a church in the New Testament." But Ketcherside, Garrett, Allen, and all others who air these hobbies should know that in Rom. 1:15, the apostle Paul said, "So, as much as in me is, I am ready to preach the Gospel to you also that are in Rome." That letter was written to the saints—therefore, the church—in Rome. So, Paul said that he was ready to "preach the Gospel" to the church in Rome! In the same book, Ketcherside argued (pages 20-21) that, since Thayer defined the Greek word from which we have the English evangelist as "a bringer of good tidings," the evangelist must travel from place to place in order to do that, and cannot thus "evangelize" by preaching in one place, to a church already established. He makes two mistakes:

d. A man might preach in one place for 20 years and be a bringer of good tidings. In practically any church assembly to which he regularly preached, there would always be the unconverted, the unsaved, those out of Christ. And in 1 Cor. 15:1-4, the apostle Paul said, "Now I make known unto you, brethren, the Gospel which I preached unto you..." By letter he was "bringing good tidings" to a church to whom those tidings had already been brought! If that could be done by letter, it would be equally possible by his preaching in person.

e. The Greek word from which we have our English evangelist and by which Ketcherside tries to prove his point, comes from a word which means, according to Thayer's Greek-English Lexicon, page 256, "to proclaim good tidings; spec. to instruct (men) concerning the things that pertain to Christian salvation...spec. to bring to one the good tidings concerning Jesus as the Messiah: (Gal. 1:8; 4:13; Rom. 1:15)." Thayer, a New Testament Greek authority, thus uses Rom. 1:15 as an example of one as an evangelist preaching the Gospel, and the apostle Paul uses a form of that same Greek word to show that he was ready, willing, and wanting to preach the Gospel to a church.

Yet, Ketcherside, Garrett, and people of like persuasion say that in the New Testament, "there is no record of anyone preaching to a church." Well, Paul said that he stood ready to do it. According to these hobby-riders, who bind laws where the Lord has bound none, an apostle was willing to do something that the hobby-riders today say should not be done. How long he would preach to that church, and the arrangements made for "the deal," were all matters left to the expediency of the churches and preachers involved

Hence, the objection to having an evangelist employed to preach regularly for a church where there are elders is not a scriptural objection, for an evangelist under an eldership is simply a preacher of the Gospel, or the Word, under an eldership. And, instead of this plan of congregations employing preachers to work full time with them stifling development, it is promoting development. Many of the congregations have classes to train the men—old, mature, young, and boys—in all phases of church edification, work, preaching, teaching, etc. And the preachers are the very ones, under the oversight of elders, who are working diligently and persistently to develop the brethren in public worship and work. Actually, the elders can feed the flock and also have the assistance of as many preachers as wisdom and ability permit. Further, Acts 13:1 names "prophets and teachers" in the church at Antioch. Young's Analytical Concordance defines the word for prophet as "public expounder." Bagster's Analytical Greek Lexicon defines the word in the Greek as "in the New Testament, a divinely commissioned and inspired person" and "a person gifted for the exposition of divine truth." The old Edward Robinson Greek and English Lexicon defines it thus: "a class of instructors or preachers who were next in rank to the apostles and before the teachers." Thayer's Greek-English Lexicon says, "In the New Testament, one who, moved by the Spirit of God and hence his organ or spokesman, solemnly declares to men what he has received by inspiration..." Here we have a number of preachers at one place, ministering to the Lord, according to vs. 2. We know nothing about the elders or their work. While the text does not affirm that there were elders there, it would be more logical and natural to assume that elders were in that church, in view of the age of the church, the speed with which elders customarily qualified in that day (e.g., Paul's first evangelistic journey in Acts 13 and 14, and 14:23), and the importance of that congregation as the launching point for Paul's three great evangelistic journeys and the reporting place for two of them. Then, in 1 Tim. 1:3, Paul wrote to Timothy, who was preaching in Ephesus. That was four or five years after the conference Paul had with the Ephesian elders, in Acts 20. Since there had been elders there four or five years before, it would be logical to assume that there were elders in Ephesus when Paul wrote 1 Tim. and instructed Timothy to preach there. Since that had been the condition, the burden of proof would be on the deniers to prove that the condition had changed. So, obviously, here we have a case of a preacher preaching in a church where there were elders.

4. "New Testament preachers had no agreement as to a stated salary, and they were to 'plow in hope.' (1 Cor. 9:10)." We have no way of knowing what agreements they had as to support, and we do know that preachers were to "live of the Gospel." (1 Cor. 9:14) This "no salary" argument is another instance of people making assertions without New Testament evidence. Roman Catholics habitually use the same method to prove their doctrines. In the final analysis, a preacher can have a stated salary agreement with a church and still "plow in hope."

5. "The average church of Christ preacher today is simply a denominational pastor." The two are not parallel. For example, "our" preacher:
   a. Is not in charge of the church.
   b. Is not the head of the church.
   c. The church is not "his charge."
   d. Is not paid to do all of the work, or even all of the preaching, for others usually are developed as they

e. Disavows the name and teaches that the elders are the pastors.

II. What is the place of the preacher in the congregation?
   A. He actually "labors in word and teaching," to use an expression from 1 Tim. 5:17, but without the office and authority of the elders mentioned in that Scripture. I am not suggesting, therefore, that this Scripture was spoken to preachers, as we are using the term in these lectures, for it certainly was applied to the elders, or overseers, of a church. But that term, "labor in the word and in teaching," certainly expresses the New Testament doctrine as to the primary function of a preacher. See Paul's instruction to Timothy, in 2 Tim. 4:1-5. So, with all of our varied duties, let us not forget or be drawn away from the first and principal task of a preacher—and that is to preach! Through the years, I have studied the overall mechanics of developing a congregation, trying to train myself in all phases of its work and details—but I have steadfastly kept before myself the idea that I am to be primarily a preacher. That is your first and most important place in the congregation. Be as good as you can in all of the business of the church, in training, developing, visiting, living close to the people and helping them with their problems, but don't go through life as a preacher of little power and interest. Let that be your No. 1 place in the church.
   B. He devotes full time to all phases of the work—to develop the church in life; to help train leaders and speakers; to stimulate the church in being a radiating center for the Gospel; to help develop all members of the congregation as "personal workers;" to convert aliens to Christ; to let the community feel the full impact of his personal influence for the Gospel, as he comes in contact with all people.
   C. He supplements the work of the elders, since generally they work at a secular trade, and they cannot devote full time to the work. He does not take over or do the elders' work, but does his own work. Actually, it is much of the type of the work that would be done by elders if they were devoting full time to the church's affairs. Keep often before the church that you are not, then, displacing the elders, but adding your labor to theirs. Making this

clear to the church will help you to keep your place; the elders not to misjudge your zeal, the church not to be confused as to the relationship between preacher, elders, and church, and will really have a tendency to encourage more work by the elders, regardless of how much you do.

D. He helps to coordinate the work of the whole church. This does not mean that you are to think of yourself as a superintendent of the church. But, the preacher naturally has more time to devote to the work. The members can quickly reach him, if he stays in as close touch with the work as he should, whereas many elders have a secular work which forbids any attention to or contact with church people while the elders are on their jobs. Too, since the preacher is generally more familiar with all details of the work, and also better acquainted with the whole congregation, naturally the people turn to him more quickly when various problems and details need extra counsel or personal attention. All of this of necessity forces the preacher into the role of a work coordinator—without in any sense detracting from the dignity and authority of the eldership.

E. He stimulates, or helps to "sparkplug," the work of the congregation. In an automobile motor, the spark, caused by the sparkplug, created in the distributor, and sent to the sparkplug, ignites the gas vapor in the cylinder, creating an explosion forcing the piston down. That turns the drive shaft, keeping the pistons going up and down. This rotating process is what causes the motor to operate, the car to run. I am not suggesting that a preacher, to do his most effective work, must always be creating explosions—though sometimes that will be the effect of your preaching! But as the sparkplug is necessary to produce the spark which ignites the gas and causes action, so do I think of the work of the preacher as producing action in a church. Certainly the type of eldership will determine the type of a church, but the type of eldership will determine the type of preaching employed by that church. So, without being offensive, smart-aleck, or a common agitator (all of which we should strive to avoid), think of the work of a preacher as the stimulator, stirrer, "sparkplug" in getting work done in a church.

F. He has two very important advantages over most of the other members.

1. He is a "specialist," in that he has made a special study and has been especially trained for that work.
2. He has full time available to devote to the work.

G. But the preacher must keep constantly in mind that he is under the oversight and discipline of the eldership, just as are all other members—deacons included. (A strange idea possesses some people: that deacons are not under the authority and oversight of the eldership, whereas all members of a congregation—deacons and preachers included—are under that eldership oversight. It is true that 1 Tim. 3:8-13 and Phil. 1:1 clearly show that in the New Testament church, there is a separate office of the deaconship. Since specific qualifications for deacons are given, to say nothing of other New Testament evidence, there you have sufficient proof for their separate existence. But no Scripture gives them any authority equal to, comparable to, separate from the elders—or authority, as such, period! Whatever authority deacons have is that as "servants," assistants to the elders, and such work entrusted to their care as the elders may delegate. If elders are so slovenly as not to map out specific responsibilities for the deacons, whatever work the deacons may "on their own" find to do, as any Christian can, they still do that work without "official authority." The elders may counsel and meet with them often or regularly—but the elders retain the oversight of the church.) Though he devotes full time to the work, and has been especially trained for it, his training, time, ability, and influence do not justify him in taking charge of the church. If there are elders, that is their function. (Acts 20:28; 1 Pet. 5:1-4) If there are no elders, he should work intensively to develop men who can be so appointed. Because the preacher is, as I said, a "specialist," peculiarly trained for this particular job, and has full time available to devote to the job, he should not adopt the air—or even feel—that he alone knows all there is to know about the work of the church. Certainly a carpenter who is efficient knows more about his work than one not trained in that field. So with an automobile mechanic, a salesman, an electrician, etc. But they can pick up information from others. So can a preacher. And if the preacher knows that, because of his training and experience, he knows more about a certain phase of congregational work (such as Vacation Bible school,

Sunday Bible school, operation of church budgets, etc.) than anyone else in the congregation, others may know as much, or more, about people, and he will do well to listen to others and avoid the appearance of "Mr. Know-It-All." And there are little people in churches, knowing little or nothing of church work, who resent one who knows more than they do and who can do a better job at anything. So, be careful how you handle this wonderful place you have in the Lord's congregation.

III. Your attitude toward acquiring such a job.

Before seeking such a place with a church, you should be very careful that you have a Christian attitude as to why you want the job. Is it because you simply want a comfortable position, with good pay, and a pleasant house? God forbid. If that is your principal aim, you will go through life on that basis, and will meet Christ in judgment as a commercialized and professional clergyman, instead of an unselfish, Christ-serving Gospel preacher. Or, is this your attitude: "Where can I be the most useful and do my best work as a Christian, in a job most suited to my ability?" If that is your attitude, you are on a sound basis. The other attitude will cause you to color all of your decisions, moves, and policies in line with your strictly material aim to "make a living." Your attitude toward this question will determine your treatment of your job, including all issues, through life. Here is the battle ground between professionalism and consecration. Settle this point before you become a preacher.

IV. A particular question to be settled at the beginning of your work.

Young preachers will early face this question: "Since I am here, not to run the church but to help it to run, should I attend the business meeting of the elders and deacons?" The answer to that problem will depend upon several factors. In case of a separate elders' meeting, attend if you are invited. But, if elders pursue a policy over a period of time of not having you in meetings, then I would recommend that you quietly obtain another job where the elders wisely see the need of working more closely with a preacher. In case of a separate deacons' meetings, attend if you are invited. If there are meetings of elders and deacons combined, attend if invited. I am stressing "if invited," for you certainly should not force yourself upon such meetings. But, if ignored over a period of time, react as recommended in the case of a separate elders' meetings—quietly go where you can lead a normal life and work with elders and deacons who are not so jealous and conceited. If the business meetings are open to the whole church, attend as a member thereof.

I now mention one reservation. You could get into a special situation where there have been such "goings-on" in a church as to make it advisable for you to steer entirely clear of all such meetings, at least for a while. So, the answers I have given to this question apply to normal cases. But you will have to learn to adapt policy and strategy to special needs. Under normal conditions, it would be sensible, practical, and natural for the preacher to meet with the elders and deacons often or regularly. But, here is a vital caution: if you attend, do not do all of the talking. Do not do most of it. Do little of it, in the sum total of what is said. But be prepared to "open up" as needed.

CHAPTER 2
THE PREACHER'S FAMILY

1) Be yourself, but be your best

If you are wondering if "The Preacher's Family" is a subject of sufficient importance to justify an entire lecture being devoted to it, just mark this down for future reference: after you have preached for less than ten years, you will have seen so many cases of preachers being "made" or "broken" by their families, their wives and children, that you will then wonder why you ever wondered about the importance of this subject. While these talks to you younger brethren deal with the day-by-day mechanics of doing the work of a Gospel preacher, it must be kept in mind that how you are able to do that work will be tremendously affected by your families.

I. The Preacher's Family as an Example.

Rom 2:21

Of course, there is a sense in which any Christian is to be an example. "There is no respect of persons with God." (Rom. 2:11) "To each according to his several ability." (Matt. 25:15) There was a time in my earliest preaching years when I resented the suggestion that my family or I should have any more expected of us than of others. After over thirty-nine years of trying to preach the Gospel of Christ and assist in the sound building of congregations, I still believe that the Lord demands of all Christians according to the principles of the two foregoing scriptures. But I also learned, long ago, that there is no avoiding the fact that there is also a sense in which these principles are particularly applicable to preachers and their families. "Thou therefore that teachest another, teachest thou not thyself?" (Rom. 2:21) All eyes are upon the preacher, because of his position of leadership and public teaching. The same is true of an elder or deacon. The New Testament stresses the kind of families they should have. (1 Tim. 3:4, 5, 12; Titus 1:6) The necessary inference to be drawn, then, is that preachers and their families set an example, in one way or another. A rebellious, smart-aleck attitude will not help, such as, "my wife is not on the payroll." True, but your wife and children will help to make or break you.

II. The Preacher's Wife.

Let us now list a few essentials in the wife of a preacher. If she is particularly deficient in any of these, she should concentrate on improvement in said particulars. If she is strong in these attitudes, she will do well to make continued growth in their excellence. If she has all desirable characteristics to an abounding degree, she should still make a study for life in their improvement. When you marry, you will do well to keep these points in mind. It will not be necessary to append to each of these points a Scripture citation. A general knowledge of the Gospel, combined with some experience and observation will prove the importance of these qualities.

   A. She simply must be a Christian. If a preacher's wife is not a member of the church, he is handicapped, compromised in his influence, and so criticized as to render him almost useless to the church. "Have we no right to lead about a wife that is a believer?" (1 Cor. 9:5) Isn't the implication in that question sufficient proof of a divine law? Paul was arguing his right to marry, but the implication of "that is a believer" was—and is—that, if he married, it was understood that he should marry a believer. "A believer" is used here to apply to one in Christ, and not just one who believed without accepting. It therefore draws a distinction between one in the church and one out of that institution. Actually, young men, we will do well to urge that all Christians, and not merely preachers, marry members of the body of Christ. Israel was ordered of God to marry only within Israel. (Neh. 13:23-27) But Israel was a type of the church, which is conceded by all of us. If it was dangerous to the spiritual soundness of Israel to marry into another religion, and Israel is a type of the New Testament church, why isn't it just as dangerous for the church member to marry one not in the church?

Further, the prohibition against a widow marrying out of the church (1 Cor. 7:39) is another "straw showing which way the wind is blowing." Young brother, if you think that you can, as a preacher, marry one not a Christian and convert her later, just because you have noticed some other members doing so, just remember this: the overwhelming majority of members of the church marrying those not in the church never convert their companions, and in practically all cases the most faithful members of the church are observably taking less interest in the church as a result of such handicap.

B. Your wife must be in <u>unreserved sympathy</u> with your work as a Gospel preacher. That does not mean that she should blindly endorse your every act. We are human and make mistakes—a hard lesson for preachers to learn. Our wives should see and point them out. But your wife will depress you and lower your efficiency if she is not in sympathy with your being a preacher. She will lose her influence on you and cease to be the influence she could and should be if she only points out errors and never speaks of or commends the good in you. And her attitude of indifference to your preaching and being out of sympathy with your work as such will creep out into the church, in that the members will discover her attitude. That will damage her influence and yours. It will be best to have a clear understanding on this point before you marry.

C. The preacher's wife <u>should not be dominating</u>. (Eph. 5:23) If she is, you will become a laughingstock, and she will become the object of severe criticism, suspicion, and hostility.

D. She should be exceedingly <u>careful in her talk, close-mouthed</u>. Sometimes they are too free to talk church business, to tell things that should not be circulated, to criticize, and so commit themselves as to virtually commit the preachers in matters before it is time for them to speak out.

E. <u>She should be a neat</u> housekeeper. A messy, clothes-scattered, slovenly-kept preacher's house always invites and receives justifiable criticism.

F. She should be <u>economical, not extravagant</u>. This becomes increasingly important when you remember that the preacher often has financial problems which others do not have. He may make more money than do some, but his financial contributions to the church are usually so far ahead of the average member, and the public's demands upon his salary are so heavy, that he will actually make less even though he makes more than some. People, in and out of the church, are quicker to criticize the preacher's family for extravagance and debt than for almost anything else.

G. She should cultivate the ability to dress with taste—though not with flashiness or extravagance. Taste in dress is a flexible term, but the most deficient in this respect can study and improve in this respect. Her income may be low and her clothes few and old, but taste in dress will overcome these two deficiencies and win general applause. No preacher's wife need feel that she must have either the most or most expensive clothes of any woman in the congregation. If she is fortunate enough to have many and expensive clothes, she should be sensible enough not to parade them and to tone down anything that would appear to be display. If her clothes are few and cheap in cost, she should study the art of taste, arrangement, and getting the most for the money. Of course, the preacher should also observe these rules in his dress. But it just so happens that right now we are discussing the preacher's wife, not the preacher.

H. She needs to visit over the church—both with the preacher, "on her own," and with other members of the church. This will not only increase her usefulness and influence as a Christian in the direct contacts upon the people, but it will set a splendid example for other Christian women to follow, and it will greatly increase the worthwhile influence of the entire preacher's family over church and community.

I. She needs to be friendly around the church building, in speaking to strangers and to all. If a preacher's wife is a "stick" in this respect, it will react unfavorably upon the preacher, and hurt his and her influence. I know some very successful preachers whose wives are cold and snooty toward visitors and strangers—and to everybody else except to their little clique, but those same preachers would be so much more influential, and so would their wives, if said wives could bring themselves to be human, kind, attentive, and interested in people.

J. However, let us throw up this caution: <u>she should not be officious</u> in that friendliness or overdo it. There is such a thing as going to either extreme. It is a marked case of overdoing it, though the intents are usually sincere and concerned with the highest motives, when the preacher AND his wife take their stand at the exit and divide the responsibility in "shaking the audience out" of the building.

K. And the preacher's wife should <u>avoid being clannish</u>. Of course, all preachers have their close friends. But there is a difference between that and clannishness. When a preacher's wife is always seen with and "runs with" only a few, that preacher is riding for a fall. Of course, I know that some women in a church are more civil, interested, courteous, attentive, and warm-hearted than most of the women. It is but natural that a preacher's wife warm up to those women in a church who treat her as a human being, who visit her, show her little courtesies, and especially help her when her husband is off on trips. The average woman in the church will speak pleasantly to the average preacher's wife at church services, and let them severely and completely alone the rest of the time, and when they are needed most. So, it is but natural that she will be drawn to any who will show her some of the milk of human kindness. And it is proper for her—and for you—to have your special friends. But I am still stressing what you will see more wisdom in ten or fifteen years from now: see that your wife—and you—will avoid clannishness, which is a selfish projection of the right to have special friends into an extreme practice of being only with that certain few all of the time.

III. The Preacher's Children

I certainly do not claim to be an expert on this—or any other—subject. But this point is often overlooked. Now I would caution against continually harping to your children on the point that they are children of a preacher, lest they develop a complex on that subject which would be permanently unwholesome. Yet, I see nothing wrong and everything right with their gradually being made to understand that their father is a preacher, and that there is more responsibility on the whole family as a result of his career and the way that the public looks to the preacher and his family for an example. An illustration of that is seen in the New Testament teaching of the qualifications of the wife and children of an elder and a deacon of the church, as in 1 Tim. 3:4-5, 11-12. Because of the position of elders and deacons, the church looks to them for leadership and example. The New Testament plainly shows that their families have special responsibilities in setting examples. Since the public looks to preachers as it does, and since the New Testament so exalts the work of a Gospel preacher, certainly the public will be influenced by the families of preachers. If it is proper for the children of elders and deacons to be taught that such children have special responsibilities to watch their influence, and that of their fathers, by the same token preachers' children should be taught the same principle.

Two points need to be stressed. First, that they <u>should be orderly in life generally, as well as in church services</u> and classes. Children of preachers who misbehave, talk, and pay no attention, in assembly worship and in classes, will set a demoralizing example in the church and before the world. And such conduct both weakens the position of the preacher in the congregation, and also makes it more difficult for a visiting preacher to enforce discipline if he feels called upon to do so. Second, that they should not be worldly. For example, a dancing son or daughter of a preacher encourages and generates more worldliness in a church in a month than his preaching will discourage in ten years. Though there are numbers of young people in many congregations who engage in the modern dance, and though there are many elders and preachers who say little or nothing against this growing menace to the church's purity, you should not fall before that softening trend, and should see to it that your children maintain a higher standard of conduct than that found among the worldly elements. If your children are worldly, and you either make no effort or cannot enforce soundness in your own children, when a preacher comes to engage in a series of meetings where you reside, and that preacher speaks out against worldliness, his preaching will be greatly weakened. In nearly all such situations, the preaching of the visiting evangelist would be more deeply resented than normally—and the Lord knows that preaching against specific types of worldliness (such as dancing, drinking, gambling, women cheapening themselves by aping the men in smoking, dressing indecently in shorts in public, etc.) will provoke enough resentment when said preaching is presented under the most favorable conditions. But if the families of preachers so act, whenever a visiting preacher speaks out against such, people will immediately say that he is just "hitting at" his brother preacher. Then they will charge jealousy, enmity, and condemn "strife." With some people in a church, you cannot mention any of the foregoing sins of worldliness—along with adultery, stinginess in financial contributions to the Lord through the church, profanity, filthy language and jokes, and many others—without many people astonishing you by saying that you have something against them, that you are just trying to make them feel badly, and that you should not be so unkind, for with some there is just no kind way to mention any specific act of worldliness. The only way to get along with those people is to mildly preach against worldliness, but be certain that you do not say specifically what worldliness is. This deplorable condition is made many times worse when a preacher goes somewhere to engage in a series of Gospel meetings, and finds the preacher's family engaging in these specific acts—with probably the local preacher saying nothing against it. The congregation will point to the children of the preacher, elders, and deacons, and decide that if they so act, such conduct must be permissible. That will certainly help to guide the church into the paths of departure, of worldly softness, and of compromise.

IV. Some Particular Family Points That Are Often Overlooked

Some apparently "little things" have much bearing upon the influence of a preacher and his family.

A. The family should be extremely careful about attending all services and classes. You cannot have much influence in preaching to a congregation that the members should attend all services and classes if your own family does not so act. People will give you credit for being honest in your appraisal of the value of such attendance, and they will think you sincere in your desire to help them and build the church, but they will pity you for not having more influence on your own family, criticize you for your lack of discipline at home, and grow indifferent to your appeals. I have known some "big names" among us, who were splendid men in the pulpit, but whose families were irregular in their attendance of services, except the Lord's Supper, and in classes. And sometimes they are habitually absent from classes. That not only leads some people astray of truth in their thinking, but also confuses the program of the church and nauseates people toward such a family—preacher included. If a preacher would best serve a church, he will support and push the whole program of the church. (2 Thess. 2:17) And if a preacher's family would be the right kind of a family, let them stand as a unit in supporting that program.

B. Another point your families should watch will be that of getting to all services and classes on time. Of course, the most careful family can have last-minute, unavoidable and understandable delays. But there are those who are habitual, or frequent, offenders. The most able preacher among us will receive much and justifiable criticism if the family (sometimes, including himself) comes dragging in late, or at the last minute. You can't go wrong if you establish a policy of being to assembly worship or class fifteen minutes, at least, before beginning time. A wider margin for assembly worship would be even better. It matters not if you and the family are the first ones there. It will be good for the influence of the preacher's family and will stimulate more zeal by others.

C. Again, the preacher and his family should be careful about the treatment of each other in public. Of course, they should also be considerate in private. But I have sometimes noticed a carelessness on this point: a little public snappishness—and often the preacher is as much to blame as others in his family. Members will be quick to notice this, and they will do you much damage in talking. Besides, under such conditions, how much influence could you have in preaching on family kindness, gentleness, patience, consideration, etc.? And, again, the influence of such irritability by the preacher's family will promote such a disposition among the members in general. If the members of a preacher's family ever have any legitimate "beef" at each other, make a rule that such will never be discussed before others, betrayed by the public tone of voice, or shown before others on the expressions of the face. Naturally, the cultivation of the correct attitude of heart will make for the proper treatment of each other, whether in private or public.

V. A Preacher's Obligation to His Family

Because a preacher's family has a peculiar obligation, however, does not release the preacher from a profound, grave, and permanent obligation to his family. I have seen preachers go to either of two extremes. Some are so tied to and dominated by their families as to be crippled in work, and ridiculed by church and world. They can make no decisions without first consulting their families. If they do make independent decisions, the families are then allowed to veto the decisions, and people soon learn "not to ask Brother Blank for an expression on a point, until he first gets his orders from home." On the other hand, some others go to the extreme of being so detached from their families as to feel that they are under no obligations at all to said families. Some preachers, for example, seem to regard their wives as the Indians are reputed to consider their squaws. Some preachers have families only for their own selfish use when at home, and they dump the major responsibility for the families upon their wives. If a preacher is never or seldom to be at home to help his wife with the family which he helped to usher into the world, just what business does he have with a family? I have known a few preachers who filled up a residence with "little stairsteps," but who never turned a hand in helping the wife with the burdens that are "standard equipment" with those little fellows, as well as other heavy duties around the house. Of course, the preacher, like other men, under normal conditions is not to take over the housework! That is more in the woman's line. But he sometimes figures that, because he is looking after spiritual duties and the souls of a congregation, he should be freed from all responsibilities of helping with the family. He obviously forgets some Scriptures in the very Bible which he preaches, such as Eph. 6:4; Heb. 12:9; Eph. 5:25, 28-29; Matt. 7:12. Religion, young men, includes your duties toward your families. Try to avoid either extreme. Maintain an independence, but do not desert and ignore your family responsibilities.

CHAPTER 3
THE PREACHER'S LIBRARY

Make up your mind to "major" on acquiring a real library. Build a practical library of considerable size, and make that project one lasting throughout your life. And do not be led astray into losing sight of its value because you know or hear of some who have many books, but who are not educated, or because you know of some who have a very few books, but who still are highly educated and effective. If one uses that line of argument to influence you against a large library, the same line of pleading could rule out the value of attending school. A practical and substantial library can enable you to spend your life in the atmosphere of the scholarship of the world in all ages, and can increase your effectiveness by supplying you with tools with which to work. In this talk I am speaking of a religious library, though you will naturally do well not to confine yourself to religious books. We study this subject under four headings: acquisition, content, use, and retention.

I. Acquiring a Religious Library.
  A. My first and urgent recommendation would be that you have a regular program for acquiring your books. Don't buy books in a haphazard, irregular, unplanned manner. Plan that program, and then stick to it. Make no changes in that program, unless you alter it for its improvement. Forget not this: the size of the program is not nearly as important as the fact of the program, and its regular execution. Any size program, involving any outlay of money, if persisted in through the years, will

gradually build you a large and useful library. Spasmodic attention to any ambition will seldom accomplish much. It certainly will not build you much of a library, unless the "spasms" of purchases are much larger than most preachers are able to afford.

B. <u>Keep a "want list," and continually add to it.</u> Be very careful to scratch books off the list as you obtain them. Let that want list stay in a conspicuous place. Though you may smile at this, and so will I, I am nevertheless quite serious when I say: keep that "want list" in a spot convenient for your wife, children, and friends to find—especially on birthdays, and other seasons of the year when presents are given! You will be surprised how that little "maneuver" will add to your collection. They will grow weary of giving you books. But remind them that they are giving you what you want, and not what they want you to want them to give you! Always list the prices by the books on your "want list," as that will guide in how much to spend at a given time. It will not be necessary for you to spend so much time poring over that list. As you work this program out in your thinking, you will become more "book conscious" as time goes on, and you may be surprised how you can keep that "want list" up to date and with the most practical books listed with very little effort.

C. <u>Keep a book fund.</u> Be extremely conscientious in observing the following rules.
   1. Take a definite amount of your weekly allowance, and reserve it for this purpose. Whatever you budget to run the general family operational expenses for a week, add an item for your book fund. Set it aside for that—and no other—purpose. Have a family understanding that this is being kept in store for that program, and it can neither be side tracked nor borrowed for any reason short of a need involving family calamity and/or honor.
   2. The largeness or smallness of this book fund is of slight importance. The main consideration is the fact of such an appropriation. Of course, you should not go overboard and budget a sum all out of proportion to other family responsibilities. Don't be ashamed at the smallness of the weekly book fund allotment, if your income is small enough to force only a little ap-

propriation. If you set aside a dime a week, a quarter, a dollar, or whatever the amount, the fact that you are thus setting aside a definite amount weekly will guarantee the accumulation of a substantial library.
3. Start this program now; it matters not how stringent your financial circumstances might be. In a sense, you in college already have a program, in that the college demands certain books to be bought. However, over and above those requirements, now is the time to begin this special book program. So many young preachers say that they will start a program like this after they graduate from college and after their first few years of struggle, when they begin to have a better income and are in a stronger financial position. That is a mistake. Start at once. By adjusting your weekly appropriation to your ability, even if it is a dime a week, you will have begun the program. That is the important point. Then, as time moves on and you improve your financial ability, you can increase your book fund appropriations to accord with your ability. But, above all, start now.

D. In your program, buy a desired book as quickly as the needed amount is there. If you allow the fund to accumulate too much, you will decide that you need those several or many dollars for something else. Further, so many desirable sets of books today can be bought at the rate of a book at a time; others may be bought on the monetary installment plan. But you will do better to avoid that installment plan for books. By saving your weekly allotment for a book fund, you will have the cash and can buy the book as the cash accumulates. There will be enough other family items to involve you in the installment plan, without sinking your library needs into such burdens. Then, when calamity sinks one in financial depths where there is no cash for books, but only enough for survival, the buying of books can wait until the cash is again available. But if you are heavily involved in installment buying for books, the installment payments will not wait. If you are able to accumulate cash for a certain set of books, you will pay less for the set than if you buy the set at the rate of a volume at a time.

E. Seek the guidance of those who know books. Of course, as you seek guidance you will sometimes run into very sincere brethren who will seek to sell you books that have very little value. If you are not careful, you can fill your shelves with stuff like that, which you will cull in later years. Much money will be wasted, time lost, effort expended, and information damaged. Save yourself some money, time, and other damage by holding that to a minimum as you seek experienced counsel. Even after you have received such guidance, still go slow in buying those books. Be a little stubborn and flatly refuse to pay high prices for some very good books that are on the market even among our own brethren today. A number of books have had their prices unreasonably jacked up. Take a little more time; don't become so impatient, and you might find that later you can pick up a copy at a better price. It is undeniable that sometimes older men will take advantage of young men in unloading books on them. Don't take so much for granted.

F. <u>Never be satisfied with your library</u>, as long as you live. Add and cull, cull and add. Time, then, will add to the number and quality of your books. While you are continually raising the level and improving the quality of your library, it must be borne in mind that you are not simply trying to build quantity, so that you may speak of the number of volumes you have. If you start after a goal of a certain number of books, you will sacrifice quality, proper balance in spending your money, and correct motives. The size as such will take care of itself as you keep in mind the reason for your library, the needs, and good judgment in spending your money. But, nevertheless, always seek to improve that library. Let your prospective wife know that she will have to accept your library as part of the family. Those books are your tools with which you labor. As they increase, your efficiency increases, all things being equal. They will occupy much space somewhere, but they must be accepted as a necessary and growing part of your equipment. They will cost money in moving from place to place, but that must be accepted as part of the life.

In urging people to buy good religious books, I find this often happens: a brother will gradually acquire several books, possibly a set of commentaries on the New Testament by our brethren, then the Adam Clarke set on the Old Testament, a Bible dictionary, possibly even a set of encyclopedia, a large concordance, and a few others to accompany these, and then he will stop buying books, and say, "I have more books now than I can ever read, so why obtain more?" He may acquire a bookcase full of books, and he will certainly be far, far ahead of 99½ per cent of all members of the church in having religious books. But he makes a fatal mistake to stop acquiring books because he has a considerable number. Certainly you do not normally expect to exhaust any one book and be through with it. Nor will you reach the place where you have no need for more books. The point is: accumulate as many as possible, that are good, and you have them for research whenever the need arises to delve deeply into any one subject. The information, data, material, and wealth is there, and the more of it you have, the better equipped you are in the fields of investigation covered by your library. So, don't be deceived by that shallow theory that "I have more books now than I can read, so I don't need any more."

II. The Content of Your Library.

Here again we run into a wide range of different ideas. It is but natural that there would be conflicting judgment in such a matter. And again I must disclaim any feeling of being an expert in this, or any, field. Certainly I claim to have made a prolonged and searching study of the question, but the best I can do is to recommend some principles to guide you in your selection of books, with just enough mention of specific books to illustrate the principles here recommended.

A. If my life could be retraced, I would in my early days go heavy on such research material as Biblical and religious encyclopedias, Bible dictionaries, and church histories. For example, make it a point to obtain the celebrated M'Clintock & Strong Encyclopedia of Biblical, Theological, and Ecclesiastical Literature. It is out of print, but can easily be obtained by the dealers in used books. It is "tops" in its field, and conservative. The 12-vol. set, in good condition, will usually cost you from $30.00 to $50.00. Another fine one is the comparatively late reprint edition, 13 vols. of The New Schaff-Herzog Encyclopedia of Religious Knowledge. It can be bought a volume at a time. The old, out-of-print 4-vol. set of the Schaff-Herzog Encyclopedia, though not having as much material, is good, and more conservative than the new 13-vol. set. All of these sets give much material not only about matter in the Bible, but also of people, movements, etc., outside of and connected with the Bible and religion in general. For a set dealing exclusively with internal Biblical material, probably the best is The International Standard Bible Encyclopedia, edited by Orr, 5 vols. Fausett's Bible Cyclopedia is a splendid 1-vol. work, lately reprinted. There are others, of course.

Among Bible dictionaries, be satisfied with nothing less than several. The Smith's 4-vol. set is great. But don't obtain it if you get M'Clintock & Strong (see above), for there is too much duplication of M & S in Smith's. You need M & S by all means. In that case, get the Smith's 3-vol. dictionary, if possible. (Used-book dealers can get it for you). The Bible dictionary by Hastings is another splendid work, and there are others.

Go strong on church histories—about all you can accumulate. Those by such authors as Phillip Schaff, George Fisher, Neander, Mosheim, Eusebius, Trench, and D'Aubigne.

Now for a word on this point. I do not mean that you should obtain all of these books before securing others, such as commentaries, etc. But my strong recommendation is that you concentrate on this field of books first; major on these; get more of them as you start, but such of the others as you feel that you simply must have. Don't make the mistake of thinking that one Bible dictionary is enough, one cyclopedia or one set of encyclopedias, or one set of church histories. In acquiring several of each there will admittedly be some overlapping, and any one of either provides a wealth of material. But several will supply variety and comparison on many points. For that reason, as you are able, equip yourself with many books in this field. Let this be the base of your religious library.

B. Among the commentaries, by all means start with the Lipscomb-Shepherd set on the New Testament, published by the Gospel Advocate. They have all New Testament books covered except James, and presumably it will be included later. Most other commentaries are more critical, going more deeply into the fine points of the original language. But the writers of this set are our own brethren, able teachers, and you need their influence around you. Obtain those of McGarvey, Lard (on Romans), Macknight, Albert Barnes, Adam Clark, P. Schaff's four volumes on the New Testament, called The International Illustrated Commentary On The New Testament (out of print; consult used-book dealers), Pulpit Commentary, Bible Commentary (edited by Cook and out of print), Lightfoot, Expositor's Greek New Testament, just to name a few of the "musts." These are the first ones I would recommend for you.

C. Christian evidences should be in abundance. By all means get Therefore Stand, by Wilbur M. Smith; The Divine Demonstration, by Harvey W. Everest; The Bible Under Fire, by John I. Campbell (probably out of print). Above all, obtain An Introduction to the Critical Study and Knowledge of the Holy Scriptures, by T. H. Horne. This is usually called simply Horne's Introduction. It is vastly more than a book on Christian evidences. There is a book you should have, All About the Bible, by Sidney Collett, and that is exactly what Horne's Introduction is—all about the Bible. Two of the Harry Rimmer books are very good: Harmony of Science and Scripture and Modern Science and the Genesis Record. Alleged Discrepancies of the Bible, by Haley, is a must. Atheism's Faith and Fruits, by Brother James D. Bales, of Harding College, is another MUST. You will find growing value from that book by continuing study. And there has never been a substitute for The Divine Demonstration, by Harvey W. Everest. It is a solid work, and you need to study it as long as you live.

D. Buy a few—but not many—good books on archeology. This will strengthen your faith, and give you some material for some practical and useful teaching and preaching. Don't be deluded into thinking that this is a dull subject and that preaching on it will be dull. If it is, you will be dull. You will need to do some extra studying on these books, and on the organization and presentation of your material in sermons and classes, so as to prevent the subject from being tedious to audiences, which have people who do not even know the meaning of the word archeology. But real study can bring new life, freshness, and interest to the subject.

As base books, you will do well to begin with: Bible and Spade, by Stephen L. Caiger; The Bible and Archeology, by Sir Frederick Kenyon; Archeology and the Bible, by George A. Barton. Approach later books with caution, and obtain counsel in selecting the ones to purchase.

E. Polemical books should include all debates involving our brethren in any capacity, the best works defending false religions, and practically all books by our brethren exposing false doctrines. This policy will make available a tremendous amount of material for reference. Often in meeting some critical point, you will need the help of those who have met that particular point. You may find a way to improve on their strategy, or you may not, but you will at least be able to learn much from the way they did or did not meet it. For example, for years I have often consulted the Boles-Boll debate on Unfulfilled Prophecy and the Neal-Wallace debate on The Thousand Years Reign of Christ, learning much from Boles and Wallace as to how they met this heresy, and also informing myself so as to correctly represent the heretics, Boll and Neal. The Woods-Porter Debate will also be of great value to you on the orphan home question, as will the Woods-Cogdill Debate on that and the general cooperation, including Herald of Truth, question. Don't read them just once, but study them, and you will see how the anti-orphan home, anti-Herald of Truth people are simply dressing up the anti-Bible class arguments in new clothes. The more debate material you have, the better equipped you will be to study special needs, and my view is that the more you have in your library, the better it will be for you.

However, because I urge you to obtain as much of this polemical, controversial material as possible, does not mean to urge you to do your preaching in the normal style of debating. I certainly believe that religious debates have been a great contributing factor to the progress of truth, even after you discount those debates that have been without justification and poorly conducted by our own men. As long as time lasts, we should not hesitate to debate, under proper conditions and with the proper men. But the style of debating is not the style for preaching. In each case, one should conduct himself as a gentleman, of course. In a debate, even though you do your best to keep your mind on the honest people in the audience that you try to help, you cannot avoid the spirit of meeting that antagonist. Sometimes Gospel preaching will have to be of that nature. But normally, it is not that. So, I am not advising you to do all of your preaching as if you were debating, but am recommending that you assemble this material so as to have special preparation in meeting an issue.

F.. Restoration Movement literature should be a "major." Since I am discussing the justifiable use of the history and literature of the Restoration Movement in a later lecture, it will be best to refrain from going into detail on that now. But collect as many books as you can which will chart the course and give us a correct "history of the case." This should be said right here: we of the churches of Christ are the result of that Restoration Movement. It was not the creation of a new church or party, but the calling of people back to the New Testament pattern of the church. A knowledge of the history of that movement will guide us better in our own knowledge of "what it is all about" and in informing others. Hence, the value of such books. The following books rate at the top of the list in this field: The Church, the Falling Away, and the Restoration, by J. W. Shepherd; The Search for the Ancient Order, 2 vols. by Earl West; Biographies and Sermons of Pioneer Preachers, by B. C. Goodpasture and W. T. Moore; The Christian System, by Alexander Campbell. There are many others, but don't overlook these.

G. Sermon books, giving whole sermons and sermon outlines, can be legitimately used and useful, provided you study them for teaching and suggestions, and not for copying. Drive this point home to your heart: they will permanently damage or profit you, depending upon how you use them. Invest your money in the best, not the lightest. Don't rush to buy a book of sermon outlines or sermons, just because you see it flashily advertised or know the author. Sometimes to know the author is to avoid the work. Sometimes not. But the counsel of experienced men can often help you on this point. There is a definite tendency among some of our brethren to go in too much for the sermons of well-known denominational preachers. Some of them can help you, but the best way I know to lose the old "ring" that our preaching has had is to absorb their sermons into your system and turn up your modernistic nose at those of our own brethren. The New Testament remains the standard, but it can be colored by denominational trends if you are not extremely careful. It is just natural to absorb something of the sermon books you study, when you study them for the purpose of finding sermon material. If you make a practice of using the outlines of the Methodist Clovis Chappell, you will—even if unconsciously—take into your system something of his spirit. There is just no escape from that. This is not to object to buying the books of sermons by denominational men. It is to sound a caution, to object to using only their books and not those of our own brethren, and to point out the danger in denominational sermon books. Before you know what has happened, you can lose the distinctiveness for which we have been noted, and you will be preaching merely soft, sweet "nothings" which can be heard in any denominational pulpit every week.

H. In this connection, a few good homiletical books should be included. Be certain to obtain On the Preparation and Delivery of Sermons, by John A. Broadus—a Baptist, yes, but as few objectionable ideas in that book as in any book ever written by one not a member of the New Testament church. You will use it for reference for years. Secure Speaking for the Master, by our own Batsell Barrett Baxter. It is brief, but basic, practical, excellent, and has the advantage of having our own spirit.

I. As soon as possible, obtain an unabridged Meriam-Webster dictionary. It will cost plenty of money, but it is a university within itself, and is the "Supreme Court" in its field. Wait on something else, and buy this early in life. There are too many ways to enumerate in which you can use it. Yes, I remember to have said that this lecture was dealing with a religious library, and this unabridged dictionary is not strictly a religious book; but its definitions and discussions of words are so related to religion, and your choice of words in general speech and in explaining religious matters is so important, as to render it indispensable.

J. All other desirable books I would classify under Miscellaneous. If you build your religious library under these ten headings, you will have a good classification system. Constantly review it, and always know where you stand as to its content.

III. The Use of Your Library.

At this point I urge only three rules.

A. First, <u>know what is in your library</u>. This will increase the material you have available for use in study. One may overlook the fact that he has a most valuable book in his library, and at a time when he most needs that data. To know the contents of your library will also increase the speed with which you can put your hands upon that material.

   A filing card system will help you to keep track of your books. That may appear a waste of time in your early days, when your books are comparatively few, and you have no trouble in remembering what you have. You may also be convinced that you will never have one large enough to justify that expedient. But look farther down the road to the point where your library may grow beyond your present expectations. And if you expect it to grow, but think that there is sufficient time in the future for a card system, please be assured that the longer you wait, the more difficult the task will become. You will find it harder to get around to it, and, when you do, you will find the volume of work considerably increased. If you will begin your listing system in your first days, and religiously adhere to if as you buy each single book, in the years to come you will have a listing system that will have been easy, which will be complete, and which will enable you to check on a book when your library really grows large. This may save undesirable duplications later, when otherwise you may buy a second copy of a book, forgetting that you have the first. Frequent reference to your filing system will increase knowledge of your works.

B. Second, study these books, rather than just have them. Only your vanity is helped when you are chiefly content to brag about what books you have, and that damages a man. I have impressed the point that with a substantial library, you are in the atmosphere of the scholarship of the world—but you are not in that environment if you are merely surrounded by the books. You have to work long hours and with systematic, methodical procedure to absorb what is in those books, as well as to be able to throw off what is objectionable in them. Since we are in another lecture dealing with the preacher's study, we

will drop this phase of the subject right here.
C. Third, though using your library, mightily strive to retain your independence of appraisal. We should not be slaves to the authors in our library, but have them to serve us. For example, some people who subscribe for only one religious paper, in their views reflect those of that paper, and whatever position that paper takes on a question, there is where they will stand. And they are the very ones who will make the loudest noise in their party-ism. In like manner, we may read a commentary on a passage, assume the author is correct, and make up our mind without more fully studying the whole Bible evidence on the subject, and without examining a variety of commentators. Maintain your independence. Do not, then, simply reproduce your books in your sermons or classes. In fact, there are always two extremes which we should try to avoid at this point:
   1. Being too conceited to be helped by them, as some church leaders are sometimes heard to slur the use of commentaries, bragging on their ability to understand and explain the Bible without such help.
   2. Being mere figureheads in aping what your books say—even if they are our own brethren. Keeping this in mind will help you to see that your library increases this ability to go to the bottom of questions, instead of becoming slaves to what So-And-So said.

IV. Retaining Your Library.

This is more important to think of than you might realize. If you don't "take out some insurance" on this phase of your library, you will later "learn the hard way."
A. Be strict about lending a book. There are three reasons for this.
   1. A book is easier to get away than is money.
   2. The borrower will often allow someone else to have it, without saying anything to you about it.
   3. Either the original borrower forgets to whom he loaned the book, or simply neglects to reclaim it, or you forget or delay. Soon the book is either gone forever, or else abused. There is a queer streak in people about their borrowing, taking care of, and returning books. They often seem to look lightly on their obligation to return a book—and within a reasonable length of time. Books have always had the

reputation of being thus abused, but that has been because people seem to lack the same sense of honor in dealing with borrowed books as with borrowed money, or else the lenders have been more careless in lending and trying to reclaim. Probably both reasons are involved. Hence, the need for your being strict in book lending. One danger in having your books in a church office or study is that church members will sometimes help themselves to your books, in your absence, and without ever mentioning the matter to you.

B. But if you just must lend your books, keep a record as to the identity of the borrower, the book, the date, and the address of that borrower.

C. If it does not come back in a reasonable length of time, call for it. If it has been lost, do not blush to ask the borrower to replace the book or give you the money to obtain it. Right there is the danger of lending books. Public libraries do not allow certain books to leave the reading room. People think nothing of that, recognize the wisdom of the policy, and do not resent it. You might be as careful about what books you lend. For sometimes, one cannot be replaced. And some borrowers are little enough to resent you asking them to restore the books of yours which they lose. If they are that little, do not let that bluff you, but understand that such a person should not receive too much consideration. Now, young men, if you think all of this "book-lending policy" sounds too hardboiled, all I ask you to do is, just stick around about 30 years, or less, then ask yourself this question: "Was that too hard?"

CHAPTER 4
STUDY AND RELATED MATTERS

In this session we are interested in the preacher's study. Some other matters will be discussed, which should not be properly classified as study. But they are related, must be spread before you during this course of lectures, and here is the place where I am choosing to notice them.

I. **Where You Have Your Study. By "study," I mean the place where you keep your books and related tools with which you work when you do most of your studying.**
   A. Where you have that study is more important than might appear at first consideration. There are at least two reasons for that.
      1. It is where you spend so much of your time.
      2. The conditions under which you study have so great influence on what you produce from your study.
   B. Now, let us acknowledge this: where you have your study is largely determined by two factors.
      1. There are <u>personal tastes</u> of preachers, which naturally vary with people.
      2. Too, <u>circumstances at different places</u> determine a decision on this point. The type and size of residence, whether owned by you or the church, its location, will all bear upon this. The same is true of the church building, and whatever, if any, space is provided there for that purpose. Consequently, no hard and fast rule may be adopted. In view of that, I want to point out advantages of having your study at the church building, and then at your residence,

for there are advantages and disadvantages at both locations.
C. Here are the advantages of having your study at the church building.
  1. It <u>releases</u> that much room at your residence from "<u>the clutches</u>" of <u>books</u>, and often adds to the attractiveness of the residence—depending upon how you keep your study.
  2. It probably <u>makes you more available to the public</u>, if you and the church consider that an advantage. But in my judgment, the church who wants a preacher to keep "office hours" has a very poor conception of the work of a Gospel preacher. Some, however, do consider this an advantage—and there is no denying that it makes you more easily accessible to the public. Occasionally—but only occasionally, thank the Lord—do we hear of church leaders who want preachers virtually to "punch a clock." If those poor, deluded, uninformed souls who think a preacher must "punch a clock," or keep "office hours," could really know the life of the average preacher with a church, they would know that a preacher would save time if he really could confine himself to such a schedule. Their idea seems to be that he must "punch a clock" in order to give the church its time! They do not know that he is subject to call 24 hours per day, is called at all hours of the day and night, that he cannot leave his job at the office or plant, as do many members of the church, but has as nearly an all-the-time job as there is—with the exception of a busy doctor who also makes house calls, or a teacher borne down with endless out-of-classroom activities. "Office hours" for preachers are often really just an excuse for people to needlessly take up the time of a preacher when he should be studying. When they have real problems, or want to visit, let them come, and they are appreciated by all of us. But there are many who abuse the privilege into the mere killing of time.
  3. Sometimes this arrangement makes your work of studying easier than at home, particularly if children are allowed to interfere. However, this should not have so much bearing upon the issue, unless you and

your wife are poor disciplinarians, and/or if you are more "jumpy" around children than a man should be.
4. Then, too, it might be embarrassing not to use the study at the church building if the church provides one—and especially if it is an up-to-date one. Always guard against this, young men: never be or appear to be ungrateful for what the church does for you. You do not always have to accept every idea the brethren advance, even if they are sincere in wanting to make life more pleasant for you, because they sometimes do not realize what mistakes they are making and how the thing they are doing is the very opposite to what any preacher would want. But you certainly do not want to appear ungrateful, even if you must respectfully and firmly decline their offer.
5. Many students of family life think that it would be well for a preacher to maintain his study at the church building, rather than to spend so much time at home. The thought is at least worth your consideration, the idea being that it would be better for both the preacher and the whole family if he led about the normal life of the average man, in being away from home at his office—at least part of the time (some preachers remain in the church office in the mornings only), and at home in about the same proportion as other men. This, of course, is a problem for each preacher and his own family, but is thought by many to be justification for a preacher maintaining his study at the church building.

D. Next, consider the advantages of having your study at your residence.
1. There you have quicker access to your books at all times. Often you will find yourself wanting to spend a short time that is available in some special study. You might need certain books. If they are at the church building, and you are some distance from there, that would be less convenient and more time-killing than if they were at your residence. I have heard some few say that, if they have their study at home, they will spend all of their time in the study and no time with the family. Well, if you are not man enough to control that, you do not need a study anywhere—what you need is a guardian!

2. Brethren are less liable to borrow—and lose—your books if you keep them at home. However stout a control you keep on that would-be plague to a preacher's library, you will still find it easier to control if your study is at home. Brethren seem to think that if a preacher's study is at the church building, since the building is owned by the church, the study or preacher's office is public property, owned partly by all members. Hence, they sometimes will ask about taking out one of your books, and ask in such a way that it will be difficult to refuse. Sometimes they will take out a book without asking, or later telling. Since they associate the book with "public property," they then seem to think nothing of re-lending your books and saying nothing to you about it. And they will usually keep your book until you are forced to ask for it. That often causes trouble.
3. Brethren—and the general public—are less likely to kill your time if your study is at home than if it is at the church building, where they feel that you have an "office." People almost universally have not the slightest conception of the life a preacher leads, of his multitude of duties. The very "character" who insists that a preacher should "punch a clock" would be the first one to gripe if he did so. Now, if someone needs you, you are glad to see him, to be of any assistance, and he can always find you through your residence if he wants to make the effort. But where you have an "office" in the church building, where you try to do your major studying, there are those who drop by just to kill time, and thereby ruin a period of concentrated study. That can be controlled better at home. I really believe that in most places, it is well for the church to maintain a general church office, to be used for the general work of the church as may be desired. But that is a far cry from the preacher having his "private office" at such a public place, just to please the fancy of those who think of the preacher as their flunkey, and who want to use his office as a loafing or time-killing place. And there will always be well-meaning brethren who have not the slightest conception of how a preacher spends his time. They may have known a very few who kill time, play

around, and do little. But, if so, they do not know that the average preacher spends more of his time, day and night, on the job than those of any profession; that he is subject to call twenty-four hours per day, seven days per week; and that he studies his Bible in preparing for a class or sermon more for that one task than the better-than-average member spends in study for a week; and that many members try to unload on preachers various errands which they should personally run. Of course, you can have much to do with controlling those who would waste your time at a church office or study. Even so, it will prove more difficult to cope with chronic loafers and "getters-off-their-chest" characters with your study at the church building than at your residence.
4. You will also find that you can handle interviews with women with more propriety at home, with your wife present or at least "in the vicinity." It can be done, of course, at a church office. But it is my conviction that, all things considered, it will be easier at home and with less chance of misunderstanding. And never treat lightly this point: a preacher cannot be too careful about matters of this sort.

II. **The Work of Studying.** *#1 WORK → AS PREACHER*
  A. This is so important that it would be most difficult to exaggerate it. It is your number one work. If you think that preaching is your number one work, I agree. And I deny that the two statements are contradictory, for the proper preaching demands most diligent study. It matters not how diligent and effective you are at visitation, promotion, engineering, and other details—your big job is studying.
  B. Study does not appeal to a lazy man. If you are thinking of men you know, who are tireless physical workers, but who will not study, do not forget that study is harder work than manual labor. It is more difficult than hunting, fishing, golfing, etc. It is the disciplining, control, direction, harnessing, and application of the mind, holding its attention to a given subject until certain objectives are realized. That puts some people to sleep.
  C. In your study habits, above all considerations, do not wait until that "last minute" to make preparation for your ser-

mons and teaching of classes. Probably, this warning will be more timely as you grow older in the work, for then we find some who get busy with other matters, postpone until the "zero hour" their preparation, and then fall back on information acquired in the past. Any preacher with much experience can do that, but it is exceedingly dangerous, to say nothing of being otherwise harmful. All through life, make it a rule to be constantly preparing, and never delay until the last few available hours. That should be done first and early. So many things can happen to you in that last minute. And a series of circumstances can combine, concentrate, and pile up on you. Then, before you know it, matters crowd in which have to be attended to then, and you are drowned in needs for which there is not enough time.

Suppose, for example, you have waited until Saturday to prepare that sermon, or class—or both. Suddenly, there occurs in the congregation a death, or major accident, a case of critical illness, other emergency calls, or prolonged "drop-in" visits. Any one of these possibilities, or a combination of them, can necessitate your presence and much of your time. Before you realize it, that last day has been partly or largely or wholly ruined as to available time. If you sit up half the night on Saturday, then, to make preparation which should have been made before, your rest has been ruined, and you are not in good physical condition for Sunday. If you fall back on the reservoir of old sermon outlines, and you make hurried preparation of one of them, you have seemed to escape that present emergency, but you have damaged yourself in lack of real, creative preparation, in contributing to a pattern of preparation that will be damaging, and shortchanged the people to whom you preach or for whom you teach.

You may be old enough in years and so stocked with information and brains that you can prepare a sermon or class on short notice. But it is unmitigated conceit if you fall back on that through laziness and failure to prepare earlier in the week. An emergency can come to any preacher or teacher, in which case you will be justifiably forced to fall back on such preparation. But to do this often, and to fall into a practice of frequently using this method—either because of laziness or unsystematic planning of your time—is but to build yourself to the place late in life where you will be shallow, giving the people a very light diet! And, if you are one of those geniuses who can go through life using this last-minute, brief preparation plan, you are to be congratulated at having such a mind, but your conceit is showing! And you still could give the audiences and classes more useful preaching and/or teaching by making your preparation early. Then, when you have extra time at the last of the week, there are many fine ways in which you can use it, and you will not be under so much strain and stress, even to the point of that eventually showing itself on your health. There will be enough affairs in the life of a preacher to add strain to you, without compounding any unnecessary complications which could have been avoided by an earlier beginning to prepare your sermons and classes.

D. Your time should be budgeted for study. You have to make an orderly arrangement of that, just as you do your monetary income and outgo. In the case of your personal financial budget, the budget will require certain latitude of allotments, and some expenses cannot be fixed. For that reason, you have classifications which provide for that, as well as for unforeseen emergencies. You had best budget your study time in the same way. After you make the most careful plans, there will be interruptions—some useless, some justifiable. That is where the man suffers who waits until the last moment to prepare.

Here is a suggestion. For a general system, you will find that you will do your best work if you arrange your mornings—starting early—for study, afternoons for visits, nights for church services, classes, and your family. There will necessarily be variations in that. Funerals, weddings, emergencies, urgent sick calls, your own family affairs, and various situations will force you to deviate from that plan. But that still will be a general plan for you to follow. You will be fresher for study in the mornings. Visits usually can be better made in the afternoons. Early rising and avoiding being a "night owl" will give you needed rest and enable you to study when your mind is at its best. If you will zealously seek to pursue this plan for your work, the more effort you concentrate on it through the years, the more success you will find yourself having in achieving these systematic goals.

E. Some sacrifices will simply have to be made for study. If you and your family are not willing for some study sacrifices to be made, you need to relinquish preaching and go into secular work. And if you engage in secular work and also preach, either irregularly or regularly, you will yet need to establish regular study habits and be willing to pay the price. The man who will take considerable preparation into the pulpit and class will, as a rule, last longer, and certainly will feed the people more solid food which will profit them. He will also be in better condition, as to stored information in his mind, when he does find himself "on the spot" sometime, with a speech to be delivered and little time to prepare.

III. Memorizing Scripture.

I cannot avoid urging you to memorize much Scripture, as long as you have any memorizing powers. There is definitely a drift away from this practice. I freely grant, if this point is urged in rebuttal, that there was a time when men quoted too much Scripture in a sermon, and almost literally smothered their audiences with Scriptures multiplied. There is such a thing as going to an extreme in that. It leaves an audience properly impressed with the ability of the speaker to memorize (and I certainly cannot recommend that as a consideration)—but with too much of a load to carry. Better it is to use fewer Scriptures, and thoroughly analyze and explain them, than to bury your hearers in an avalanche of passages too numerous to be retained. Still, when all of that is properly considered and duly accepted, the fact remains that there has been of late years too much of a swing away from memorizing Scriptures and quoting them in sermons. And there are at least four distinct values attached to considerable memorizing of Scriptures.

A. It will increase your knowledge of the Bible—both in acquisition and retention.

B. It will give your mind quicker access to the whole Bible in collecting sermon material. When studying for a sermon or class, Scriptures that you have previously memorized will suddenly focus themselves upon your memory.

C. It will give you splendid mental discipline. That is desirable and necessary, of course, and what better agent could one use than the Bible to achieve that discipline?

D. While the public reading of the Scripture is not to be

lightly esteemed, quoting Scripture in a sermon will more securely obtain and retain audience interest in your speech. There should be much public reading from the Bible, with the Bible in your hand and plainly visible to the audience. Such observation makes for greater reverence for the Book and respect for what you say, as well as helping the audience to make the connection between the Book and God. But some men seem to overlook that too much reading becomes tedious, even in the best of readers. I fear, too, that memorizing and quoting Scriptures are unpopular with some because they are reluctant to engage in the mental work necessary for such. The tendency to get away from memorizing Scripture and quoting references is a weakening trend and not a strengthening virtue.

IV. Citing Scriptural References in Sermons.

Gospel preachers have long been distinguished for citing Scriptures proving their points, giving "book, chapter, and verse." But we are positively appalled at the drift from that. All too often we hear today: "The Bible says." Well, why not tell your audience where the Bible says it? That is what the church grew on in this country, and it is too lamentable for words that there is a tendency away from this. Now, citing your reference has at least five advantages.

A. First, it inspires audience confidence in the speaker's reliability.
B. Second, some will remember at least some of the references and be better able to check on special points.
C. Third, others will record all or some of your references. I uniformly see that done. So do many other preachers. Why not, then, make it easier for your conscientious and inquiring hearer to check up and see for himself that what you preach is true?
D. Fourth, it will train your memory of these particular passages, just as repeating a name in conversation helps to stamp that name on your mind.
E. Fifth, it will thus discipline your mind and strengthen it for later years.

V. Use of Your Outlines.

A. Outlining your sermon has three points in its favor.
   1. The organizing of your thoughts. That is too obvious to admit of any debate.

2. Helping to deliver your sermons in a more logical manner. So, outlining your speech helps the speaker.
3. Helping the audience to retain the thoughts you present. Now, you may be thinking of some genius who usually or often speaks without any prepared outline, who "scatters around" as to points, but who holds audiences spellbound and ranks as an outstanding speaker. Don't be misled by the few individuals of that type whom you may know. Because there may be a few exceptions to this rule, that does not properly encourage the average speaker to disregard outlining. The "genius" of whom you may be thinking may impress audiences by his platform ability, but that is usually as far as it goes; he will not leave his audience with any connected train of thought or any orderly recollection of the points made. The preacher better serves his audience who may not be so outstanding in ability, but who presents an orderly arrangement of points for their present impression and future study. Therefore, study the science of outlining. It will be a subject for study throughout your life, will improve your preaching, and will help your audiences in their first impressions and future memories.

B. Strive for the utmost simplicity in your outlines. An outline can be made so detailed and full as to be tedious and burdensome. Simplicity of plan will call for more thinking on your feet and will aid a clearer mental grasp of the sermon.

C. But, do not be wedded to your outline during delivery of your sermon. If you cannot get your sermon outline into your mind, when you are its author and creator, how do you expect the audience to grasp and retain it? Too much dependence upon your outline during your sermon will weaken you in presentation, in thinking, and in audience effect.

D. Be particularly careful to make your own outlines; do not use "canned" ones. One of the most harmful indulgencies of a preacher is to preach another's outline in its completeness. Granting, for sake of argument, that it far surpasses one which you can create, you are damaged when you use it. Just to that extent, you retard your own creative powers, lessening your power to dig for yourself.

Other outlines can be helpful in offering suggestions, in Biblical instruction, and in observing how outlines are constructed. But that is as far as they should be used. Avoid as you would the leprosy anything that will tend to make you a copyist, an imitator, and less of a thinker for yourself. So, use outlines of others in a legitimate way, but preach your own outlines.

VI. **The Selection of Subjects.**
 A. In my first few years of preaching, I thought it best to preach to the church in the morning services and to the world at night. I had something of the old distinction—obtained from some old college teachers—between "Divine worship" and "Gospel meeting," morning and night, respectively. But it was not long before I discovered my mistake. In both services, we worship the Divine God and the Gospel is preached, if we are faithful to the New Testament.
 B. Let me suggest five reasons why we should vary the emphasis of the Sunday morning and night sermons, sometimes following my first procedure, sometimes reversing it, sometimes combining the two at either or each service. 1.
    1. Audiences change, in their normal movement. Occasionally they are practically the same each time, but only rarely is that true.
    2. In some places we really have more outsiders visiting our morning services than the night ones.
    3. Shift-work sometimes changes audience complexion with regularity, yielding as many or more members in night attendance as in day services.
    4. Church families need indoctrination in those subjects which we ordinarily think of as especially needed for the world.
    5. The world needs to hear more sermons than it often does concerned directly with Christian duties, to understand that the Gospel demands certain standards of life and work of the Christian. For these reasons, sometimes preach on "Baptism," "The One Church," etc., on Sunday morning; sometimes on "Prayer," "Love," "Purity," etc., on Sunday night. Try to be a balanced preacher, not infatuated with one subject or one type of subject.
       Now, put this to a practical test. Suppose that your

Sunday morning sermons are habitually "to the church." You edify the members of the congregation in the Christian graces, deepen their scriptural feeling, influence them to be more liberal, mold them into a close bond of unity, impress them with the non-worldly character of Christians, fire them with enthusiasm, stir them to be more benevolent toward the unfortunate, persuade them to send more preachers to foreign countries and areas in our nation where the church is weak, lead them to greater accomplishments in contributing to Christian colleges, homes for homeless children and the aged—and on and on in the field of good works. Well, if you can do all of that, you might feel that you have a church after the Lord's New Testament pattern. Not necessarily. In those particulars, yes. But you have left a gaping weakness. You have omitted teaching them the difference in the church which Christ established and humanly-originated denominations of men. You have failed to teach "first principles" and to let them know that there is just one way to be saved, and just one church in which salvation is—and churches of Christ happen to represent that body. You have failed to arm them against meeting false doctrine, failing to point out that the New Testament church can have no fellowship with human sects. They have not been indoctrinated in the militant spirit of Christianity as it contends against all errors of human bodies and origin. They have been led to believe that Christianity is all sweetness and no war against errors of doctrine, that "we" are nearer the truth than others, but "other churches" can also be saved, and they really do not know the distinctive position of the church in contrast with denominations. They have been led to believe that Christianity is all positive and not negative, that we oppose nothing!

"But, wait," you say, "I attend to all of those matters you think I omit, in my Sunday night preaching." Fine. But usually about half of the church is there. So many never hear those Sunday night lessons so desperately needed. Half the church and its children and young people, then, grow up never knowing but one side of your preaching. It is, thus, a half-taught

      church. You can see, therefore, the need for balancing, mixing these subjects between Sunday morning and night.
- C. As subjects or brief outline thoughts come to you, jot them down. Then, expand as soon as you have time, and before they get away from your fresh enthusiasm as to that thought. If you will follow this as a rule, you will be surprised how much sermon-outline material this will make available to you.

CHAPTER 5
RECREATION AND RELATED MATTERS

MARK 6:31

The problem of recreation for a preacher is probably not of such gravity as to demand an entire lecture on the subject. On the other hand, it is worthy of more serious study than it often receives. Personal tastes, and even abilities, are so essentially involved in this question that I almost shrink from such a discussion. But there are enough angles, advantages, and dangers in a preacher's recreation to warrant this attention. Then, there are other problems, more or less related to recreation, which we shall examine in the same talk.

I. **Recreation in General.**
  A. There are several legitimate forms of recreation. Recreation does not consist merely in ball games or fishing. Variety is basically in the nature of recreation.
    1. Among the forms of recreation, which are proper for a Gospel preacher, are to be found hunting, fishing, golf, ball games (both as a spectator and player—if the "preacher-player" will keep his age in mind!), gardening, vacations, attending Christian college lectureships, various and sundry short trips, etc. I know of no reason why any Gospel preacher should feel that any of these activities should be considered "out of bounds." Occasionally we encounter a Gospel preacher who thinks that a preacher should not attend ball games, but he loves to hunt or fish! We preachers can be the most inconsistent of creatures. One man thinks it terrible to drink coca colas, but

loves to gulp coffee as I do—and that is plenty!
2. These, and other, forms of recreation are <u>not only legitimate, but are helpful, if properly used.</u>
    a. In the first place, they are beneficial to the preacher. They give him relaxation, and that means renewal of strength. It is a question of variety versus rut. Sometimes we wait too late to give attention to such matters. Vacations especially are neglected. That preacher is doing more harm than good in the long run who engages in a protracted meeting on his vacation time. Unreasonable people sometimes criticize a doctor for "taking off" and completely separating himself from his patients. What they ignore is that there is a limit to which he can go; he may by that absence be denied to a call that is urgent, but that rest may so refresh him as to keep him longer in the harness; he may in the long run, though working a hardship on an urgent caller, be able to serve more people, for a longer time, and in a better way. Remember that when you load up your vacation time with a meeting, even though the call is from some church urgently needing you, and/or you may stand in need of the extra income, try to take a long-range view of such problems. Often young men, because of their youth, vigor, and ability to stand more pressure than men of age, will think that vacations are useless extravagances in the early years of their careers, but that they will get around to such "frills" in later years when they are needed. They are too strong for such! Vacations are for sissies and idlers. But a wise doctor will tell you that your treatment of your body in early years (such as in allowing time for vacations, cautioning against too much eating, avoiding such a frenzied rush all of the time, getting sufficient rest—and especially on Saturday nights) will have much, very much to do with the condition of your body when you reach middle age or later in life. When you are in your late twenties or early thirties, it may seem foolish to you to take regular vacation periods, in which you hold no meetings and do no preaching, and especially when you feel so "fine and dandy" all of

the time. But there comes a time to many men when they wish they had started early in life the regular practice of taking vacations, completely separated from any preaching or related work, isolated from your job, and, as nearly as possible, putting it out of your mind. To get away from all of that is just as necessary for a preacher as for many in other high-pressure careers. Too much stress cannot be placed on this point. It is no credit to brag, "I have never taken a vacation."

b. In the second place, actual recreation comes back in dividends to the congregation. Whatever refreshes the preacher will improve his work, and the congregation will correspondingly benefit. That is why congregations should demand that their preachers, with their families, take regular vacations. If churches are so selfish and shortsighted as to ignore this, or to refuse to pay a preacher while on vacation, it is up to the preachers to teach them out of this miserly and miserable narrowness. Very few of the brethren will do it for you. I agree that it is embarrassing, that good taste must be kept in view, and your "good should not be evil spoken of." But still it should be done. For example, a preacher who attends college lectureships will be so improved in knowledge and ideas, and so renewed in strength, that the congregation will in turn be so benefitted by making it possible for him to go. Because some abuse this privilege by trying to attend too many such programs in a single year, by making it an occasion for "politicking," making contacts for jobs—immediate or future, by seeking publicity, etc., should not drive you to the other extreme of indifference to such values. Further, the colleges, because of the service they render, are due our interest. And the more we attend, the better posted we are on the spirit and attitude of the schools, making us better prepared to guide young people and parents in their selections. After all, we are furthering the progress of the Gospel and the church when we throw the full weight of our influence into the effort to persuade our young people to attend Christian colleges. Attending the lectureships will help you to do a better job at that endeavor, and give you recreation that will be of inestimable value to you and the congregation.

    c. A third benefit in a preacher's recreation is to his family. The family needs to have relief from the grind and to avoid the rut just as much as does the preacher. Sometimes we observe a preacher who selfishly has to have all of these outings, but who makes no provision for his family. He seems to forget that his wife and children compose essential parts of the team. And, really, the family needs to be together, off to itself, away from all others, at intervals. That not only contributes to refreshing relaxation and rehabilitation of bodies, but it is good for family relationships. Common sense should teach this. And a man's responsibility to his family demands some provisions of this sort. Many problems, which may never even be mentioned, may nevertheless be solved naturally and easily as a family spends real vacation periods together.

    d. And then, there is a fourth benefit. It is sometimes true that a preacher can use some forms of recreation as a means of influencing some alien to accept Christ, or some wayward member to return to faithfulness. It is the one way you sometimes have of thawing out a person to the point where he can be influenced for that which is right. It is one way of being in the association of various outsiders and members of the church, with the normal benefits to both preacher and people.

B. But <u>we should be careful that recreation is not abused</u>. We can go to an extreme in engaging in these pursuits just as we can in indifference to them. Recreation should not be allowed to cause our work to be neglected. A preacher should not, for example, be a hunter or a fisherman to the extent that whenever someone looks for him, he is gone. A preacher can try to "make all the lectureships," or most of them, and neglect his work. Sanity should be retained. After all, young brethren, you can stay busy and have all of the jobs you need, even if you never attend a college lectureship during your whole life. If that be a motive for attendance, you had best stay away. Recreation trips, especially short ones, are sometimes abused by preachers who take them, but who never consult the elders regarding such. Now, I am not one of these people believing in the silly and unreasonable idea of a preacher having to punch a timeclock, nor do I think that he has to ask the elders' permission for every step he takes. That would make mere foremen and dictators of the elders, and remove any initiative in the preacher. But I do believe that elders and preacher should work very closely as a team—a thought that is emphasized several times in these lectures, and a preacher has no business taking an out-of-town trip without the elders at least knowing about it. He can be urgently needed, and it should be known where he can be reached, if it is necessary to contact him. Besides, the elders are the overseers of the church and are entitled to know where their preacher is. Keep this in mind in taking your recreation trips. In the final analysis, seek proper recreation, but retain your balance, and avoid being interested in such things to the extent that you are less interested in your preaching, teaching, visiting, and general congregational promotion.

II. The Problem of Luncheon Clubs.

In some towns, where there are Rotary, Kiwanis, Lions luncheon clubs, Chamber of Commerce, and other community clubs, you will often face the problem of membership therein—especially if some member of the congregation exerts some pressure to that end. Have your convictions, and examine all of the evidence pro and con, but avoid being too dogmatic on matters of judgment such as this. Let me lay before you some evidence on both sides of the question.

    A. In favor of a Gospel preacher being in such organizations, it is argued that:
        1. They broaden the preacher.
        2. They increase his contacts, and thus enlarge his opportunities for influencing people.
        3. They improve community opinion of the church, since they think we are "narrow" at best.
        4. It is an honor for our preachers to have that recognition by being permitted to join such groups, in which the leaders of the communities hold membership.
        5. The preacher is held to be not responsible for ques-

tionable club practices, such as dances, card parties, etc. He may even register his opposition.
B. In opposition to the foregoing, it is replied:
1. Too many embarrassing questions come up for comfort for a Gospel preacher, such as dances, bridge and other gambling devices to raise money, club night at revival meetings, etc.
2. It is argued that membership in such a group carries apparent endorsement of such evils (though many worldly members, including some preachers, deny that such activities are evil), unless public exception is noted. While it is true that the preacher may record his opposition, it is difficult to inform the public sufficiently for complete understanding. And if you make your objection strong enough for the information of it to be community-wide, then you are at cross purposes with the very outfit with which you are trying to go along.
3. It is further insisted that it is more difficult for a preacher to draw the line against such worldliness when associated in group endeavor with those not in sympathy with his ideals. My own experience of three years in a Rotary club, which was very conservative, plus talking with many on both sides of the controversy of whether the preacher shall belong, plus observation of given situations, plus conviction as to Bible principles, all combine to lead me to the position that in the long run, you will do better to stay out of them. There will be less embarrassment and compromise of position for you as a Gospel preacher, and for the church. While we should not lay down as a Bible law our own views of matters so manifestly those of judgment, individual treatment, and subject to varying and local conditions, I can see no good results which come from such club membership. I have never seen or heard of any beneficial results from such—no one converted by a preacher being in such clubs, no long-range results which brought any solid and actual good to the cause of Christ in a given town. On the contrary, I have known of many, many good brethren who finally were forced to relinquish membership in such clubs because of the compromising positions in which they were so often

placed. And my observation has been that more evil than good came therefrom—to say nothing of the valuable time which might have been better spent in other channels. But, I repeat, this is a personal and local problem, and no ironclad "law" should be formulated.

III. The Amount of Time to be Away in Meetings.

In this series of lectures we are striving principally to deal with everyday problems faced by the preacher and the mechanics of doing his work. There are some of these questions which are difficult to be classed under the various headings of these talks. The problems of membership in luncheon clubs and that of how much time to be away in meetings are at least related to recreation. For that reason, they are treated in this speech.

As to the problem of how much time to allot to meetings away from your home congregation, there are many factors involved. For that reason, no ironclad rule can be laid down.

A. One extreme view is this: the church which wants its preacher at home practically all of the time. There may occasionally be special conditions which justify this, for a limited time, such as rebellious upheavals, an especially low state of affairs, etc. But for normal procedure, here is a fourfold error:
   1. It is extremely selfish.
   2. It stifles development of men within the church.
   3. It robs the church and preacher of beneficial variety.
   4. It robs the preacher of legitimate and useful contacts with congregations.

   The church needs to hear other voices. The men of the church need to have more responsibility on them and ability developed within them. The church needs to develop more appreciation for its men who supply in the absence of the regular preacher, and for others who may be sometimes brought in. There is just nothing right or beneficial in the long run in the plan of keeping a preacher at home all, or practically all, of the time. That is an extreme position that will fossilize a church and preacher. As a rule, you will help yourself in the long run if you will flatly decline such jobs, regardless of how badly you may need a job at a given time. When you work with a selfish, shortsighted group you are unhappy, out of place, and your only excuse for ever being with such a church will be the possibility of teaching them out of their selfishness and narrow boundaries. Whether you can do that will be your problem.

B. But here is another extreme. In this case, the preacher thinks that the amount of time, regardless of how much, does not adversely affect the church. He is mistaken. Why is he there in the first place? Is it just to draw a pay check when he does not want to be "on the go"? Just as you can smother, spoil, and petrify a church's growth by being there all of the time, you can also retard a church by being gone so much of the time as to create confusion, rob it of your personal attention so badly needed, and lose much material which might otherwise be saved.

C. Two general rules will help you in determining the proper balance to this problem.

1. Be away from your residence work a moderate amount of time. Of course, there is much difference of opinion as to what is a moderate amount of time. In my judgment, three or four (preferably three) meetings per year, two Sundays to each meeting, and a two-week vacation time should be ample. If the church wishes to send you on any meetings at its expense, let them not be counted in the three or four that you have in your own choosing. This is the rule which I have followed, with little variation, since graduation from college in 1924. Some think that they have to accept more meetings, else the supply of calls for meetings will dwindle. No; the meeting invitations will continue to come each year, more than you can accept, and you will stay busy.

2. Another rule is this: space out the meetings over the year, instead of bunching them. The full-time job will suffer less in that way. A long period of absence in meetings invariably causes a dip in interest and attendance. Try having one meeting away in the spring, one in the summer, and one in the fall, and you probably will see less damage to the home congregation than if you are gone six or eight weeks at a time. And by damage, I am thinking also of the fact that a prolonged absence takes you out of touch with the work to a greater extent than under the plan

of spacing your meetings. The experience of several years in helping to build congregations will demonstrate the wisdom of these rules, and you will be less influenced by the opposers who are more theoretical and opinionated rather than practical.

CHAPTER 6
SPECIAL PITFALLS
PART 1

Since we are dealing with the mechanics of doing the work of a Gospel preacher, spending your major time with a given congregation, the next four lectures will deal with what I am calling "Special Pitfalls." These are some particular dangers to the work of a preacher. Let me illustrate what I have in mind in this way: make a list of all the preachers you know who have been forced to leave a given work; list the reasons for such leavings, as far as you can ascertain; look over your list, and most of them will be one of the seventeen "special pitfalls" that will be studied in these four speeches. These seventeen dangers are the ones which most often trip preachers. Hence, their importance for study. We deal with four in this lecture. The four of this session deal with talk—three of the points with private, and one with public, talk.

I. A False Start.

The beginning of your work with a congregation is exceedingly important. The odds are nearly always in your favor. But it is possible to turn the tables—and needlessly so—by getting off to a false start. Sometimes you can never recover from such a start. In that case, it would be best to move—and fast. But such a mistake can be avoided by exercising much care in how you commence your work.

    A. For example, there is the danger of <u>too much talk</u> when a preacher begins his work with a congregation. He may be the excessive talker, in the first place. In such case, he needs to slow himself down at that point. Too, he is anxious to make a good impression, as well as being full of zeal. No, I am not advocating that he "clam up" and be like a mummy. But less general talk at first will create more respect—if it is not taken to the extreme of saying nothing in company with others, to the embarrassment of everyone in your presence. Certainly one can go to the extreme of being non-talkative. The "say-nothing" type can be a bore. He can be so much that way that people will prefer not to be with him. If he has an inferiority complex and is afraid to talk, does not know how to converse with others, then he should diligently study that art and work insistently to overcome it. So, please do not allow what I say here about loose, excessive talking to influence you to the other extreme. Just take care to be more tight-lipped than people generally are. The preacher who gains a reputation for careless, constant, excessive, loose talking will seriously cripple his influence. People will fear to confide in him or bring their problems to him. They will shun any serious discussion of issues where they would fear to be quoted. And such a preacher would have no influence in preaching to people on a text such as this: "And I say unto you, that every idle word that men shall speak, they shall give account thereof in the Day of Judgment. For by thy words thou shalt be justified, and by thy words thou shalt be condemned." (Matt. 12:36-37) In my judgment, there are few things more important in the work of a preacher than his use of his personal talking. Through the years you will be surprised at how people come to you or detour around you depending upon how careful you are in your speech with others, in just ordinary, everyday conversation.

B. You can fall into this pit of a false start by <u>saying a lot about what you are and are not going to do</u>. It is proper, of course, to discuss with people aims and plans, ideals and desires. But that should be done with care. And always keep in mind that the elders are the overseers, that you and they are on the same team, that cooperation among all of you is necessary, and that due regard for their position as church overseers is essential. It is possible for a preacher to talk about future acts, plans, aims in such a way as to impress people that he is bragging.

Run things thru the elders

C. Again, sometimes a preacher will do some loose talk in committing the church. Unless decisions have been officially made, it is unwise to be talking about what the church is or is not going to do. If you simply must give expression to such views, be particular to express it as your opinion as to what the church will or will not do, rather than making a flat assertion as to future action. But, in most instances, it is far better to refrain even from such opinions, for people may not properly quote you, and trouble will result. Caution: even when decisions have been made, how they are publicized calls for care, planning, and an understanding with all parties involved. You can commit the church to members and/or outsiders before you have been authorized to do so. Usually the result is that you, the elders, and the whole church will be embarrassed, with permanent damage done.

D. This special pitfall of a false start is sometimes accomplished by looseness of talk in discussing people. You may find yourself discussing the shortcomings of a member, and in conversation with members of the congregation who are friendly to the one being discussed. Or, perhaps the one with whom you talk will quote you, and the remarks will find their way home. After all, "chickens come home to roost." Then, you may do some loose talk in discussing preachers. They have their special friends, who will resent anything unfavorable said about them. Sometimes a preacher very foolishly engages in loose talk about his predecessor—and most of such talk is loose! You should use extreme caution in such matters, not only because you never know how and where you will be quoted and how much damage can be done in a congregation, but also because so much of this type of talking is wrong within itself.

II. Too Much Confidential Talk.

This can become a very grave pitfall.

A. Let me urge you to go very, very slow in taking people into your deepest confidence. There are at least three reasons for that.

1. Your appraisal of the person could be wrong. You will sometimes be shocked at how wrong you were in your estimate of people. I do not want you to be cynical, overly suspicious, and trustful of no one. Many, many people are worthy of your deepest confidence,

and you will appreciate that fact the more you deal with them. But many others will amaze you as to how mistaken you were about them. They make splendid first impressions. And they may deceive you for even a long time. But eventually you find that they are deceptive, not honest, are two-faced, saying one thing to your face and immediately something else to your back. They will frequently seem to be the very best people in the church. They make pious appearances and have soft voices. All of this adds up, young men, to the fact, that you will do well to be extremely cautious about confiding in and talking to people. Watch your step.

    2. The person in whom you confide can change his attitude. Here again people will amaze you! This type of a person doesn't really mean to be deceptive or hypocritical in pretending to be your friend, while all the time engaging in backbiting. But this person is more of the fickle, wishy-washy type. He—or she—will very sincerely be your friend for a while. Then something begins to work on that character; he gradually undergoes a change of attitude; then you are sorry that you placed confidence in and told certain things to that person. There are people who are noted for that. I am thinking right now of an elder in a church, not where I have ever worked full time, but with whom I am acquainted, and of whom I have certain knowledge. He has a name for taking a preacher to his heart, "eating him up," so to speak, with friendship, being for him and with him as a companion. Then some trivial something will happen (sometimes the dictates of his wife), and he will "go sour" on the preacher, turn against him, and make life miserable for him. He habitually does that to preachers working with that church, and most of them fall into his trap. It is a city-wide joke. But it isn't funny. And you had best go slowly, again, for people—even those not as extreme characters as that elder—change, and you may be sorry of your talk.

    3. You can change in your attitudes.

B. In taking people into your confidence, look to the end of your stay at a place.

    1. I do not mean by that to be recommending that all,

or any, of your acts be done with a view to making people think well of you, regardless of what is the cost.
 2. But not compromising in matters of doctrine is one thing, while judgment as to how to talk freely with people is something else. I have not one point of doctrine to yield, but freely grant that there is much to be learned by all of us as to how to talk with folks.
C. Sometimes your warmest friends will quote you at a time and in a way that will do you the most damage, without intending to hurt you. You have to have friends. It is natural to have very special friends. But they can hurt you while wanting only to help, and being careless in how they quote you. Your very best friends can sometimes do you the most damage.
D. So, I would urge this test: "Would I be embarrassed if what I am about to say became public property?" Many preachers positively destroy their usefulness in a place by too much confidential talk, and long before their period of usefulness in said place would otherwise terminate. It is so easy to do this, for human nature longs for someone in whom to confide, with whom to discuss problems, upon whom to lean for support. But being too trustful and going too far with your confidences can boomerang in a most unpleasant way. Hence, go slow in your confidential talk, lest you find that you have confided in that "double-minded man, unstable in all his ways." (Jas. 1:8). A good procedure right here is this: ask yourself some questions about what you are preparing to say to this person. "When what I am saying is known by all parties concerned, what effect will my talk have on my influence for good on those people? On other people? On my position as evangelist with this church and in this town? On people's general confidence in my soundness, spirit, sensibleness, judgment, and worthiness to be trusted?" Though the apostle Paul was not speaking of talking to other people, he was teaching on the importance of influence when he wrote: "For we take thought for things honorable, not only in the sight of the Lord, but also in the sight of men." (2 Cor. 8:21) And there is positively no way to exaggerate the effect that your talking to people in confidence will have on your influence.

III. Taking Sides in a Purely Personal Dispute.

This is what I would designate as a very special pitfall for a preacher—or anyone. It is easy to be drawn into a dispute, thinking that matters of principle are involved, when actually personal likes and dislikes are at the root of the controversy. You may not know that, and may be sucked into the pitfall. The preacher does not live who has not been deceived at this point, regardless of how piously and hypocritically some of them disclaim their guilt and proclaim their superiority. There is no need, however, for discouragement because of this general weakness. The best that any of us can do is to be especially careful at this point. That will hold the damage to a minimum. Now let us consider some good rules to assist us in being guarded against this danger.

   A. First, be doubly careful not to make up your mind about people or situations until you have heard all of the evidence. This is the principle proclaimed by our Lord in Matt. 7:1, "Judge not, that ye be not judged." He was not forbidding you to decide the guilt or innocence of one, the right or wrong of a proposition, when you have the evidence, for in Matt. 7:20, He said, "Therefore by their fruits ye shall know them." A man approaching you on the street may appear, from a distance, to be drunk. On closer inspection, however, you can know whether his unsteady walk was due to a crippled or diseased condition, a temporary illness, or if he has the known and recognizable signs of being drunk. A doctrine may, at first hearing, seem to be true, but it has to be thoroughly tested by all of the evidence of God's Word. The statement of Matt. 7:1 was simply designed to influence us to withhold judgment until all of the evidence is available and has been examined. But you need to exercise the greatest caution to know that you have all of the evidence. Here is where all of us seem most likely to err: we jump at a conclusion, assuming we have all of the data. Even after you have made an intensive and exhaustive investigation, you will often find one little particle of evidence which puts the whole matter in an entirely different light. We just cannot be too careful here.
   B. The very best of people can make these four mistakes:
      1. Be wrong in their appraisal.
      2. Be unconsciously biased—swayed by personal feelings when not aware of such influence in their judgment.

THE PREACHER AND HIS WORK

Figures don't lie, but "liars figure"

    3. Give inaccurate evidence—based on the testimony of someone judged to be in possession of the facts, when actually that informant was entirely wrong in his supposed knowledge.

    4. Sincerely lead you astray.

C. Therefore, take a long time in formulating a fixed opinion about either people or events reported to you.

D. Then remember that your "fixed" opinion about people is always subject to change, because people change, and your information could be entirely wrong. If he will tell you the truth, any veteran preacher among us could tell many interesting stories of having a "red face" as a result of trusting the "information" someone gave, of framing a course of conduct based altogether upon that information, then of learning how erroneous the "evidence" was, and finally of saying, at least to himself, "What a dope I was!"

E. Here is one situation where these principles are especially appropriate: avoid being drawn into personal disputes within a congregation, except when absolutely necessary. That is sometimes unavoidable. Sometimes your position among the people means that you can and should "move in" to help the situation. If you have to take a position as to the truth or error of a person's position in a dispute, then try to avoid being placed in the light of a partisan. So very often, someone in a congregation will ease up to you and pour into your ears a story of what someone has done or how evil that one is. You have every reason to have great trust in your informant. He may be one of the most faithful and reliable of the members. You think that he—or she—just could not be mistaken about that situation. Later, you learn that your "reliable" informant was hostile to the one being discussed, or received his information from one who was involved in a personal dispute. Your connection with the fracas became a matter of principle so far as you were concerned, but you learned that those at the bottom of it were simply personally hostile to each other, and with them it was a matter of personalities and not of principle. Over and over this will happen to you through life. And in some cases, years will pass before you have all of the facts and learn what a mistake you made. There may be little or nothing then that you can do about it. So, keep your eyes on the special pitfall for a preacher, of being drawn as a partisan into purely personal disputes—or into disputes of principle which eventuate and degenerate into disputes of mere personalities.

IV. A Fussy, Sarcastic, Smart-aleck Nature.

This manner seems quite easy for preachers to drift into, and particularly in early years. However, it is observed among veterans of many years, and it is by no means confined to young preachers. But, because of youth, lack of seasoning, and all that goes with the fire of this time of life, perhaps there is more danger of this special pitfall in early years than later in your preaching career. Some preachers seem to associate this characteristic with soundness. Such a character thinks of every sermon as "laying out" the audience, of "skinning 'em," "going after them," and terms of such import. It becomes rather difficult to counsel with and change such an egotist. Hence, young men, please be warned of this danger and examine yourself thoroughly, lest you fall into this pitfall.

A. But let us make this clear. Because I thus speak to you, some may misunderstand. Three things I am not advocating:
   1. That you cringe, cower, or crawl for fear of the frown of some soft-soaper.
   2. That you fail to be positive.
   3. That you rule all militancy out of your manner. If you think I am advising you to become such a policy man as to fail to be definite, or to fail to oppose compromising tendencies, you can check my record and where I now preach, and you will find that such is not my record and that there is no present trend in that direction. So, nothing I am recommending here is to be interpreted as favoring a softness or oppose-nothing policy.

B. But the fussy, sarcastic, smart-aleck, hateful manner is sometimes standard equipment with preachers, mature ones as well as younger ones. Since we are fighting Satan, they act as if their audiences were composed only of Satan and his disciples, of hypocrites—and they proceed accordingly.

C. The whole audience, however, should not be confused with a few, prejudiced hypocrites, if such there be in your audience. Nor should it be confused with some evil opposer who is not present. Sometimes this irritable manner in preaching is developed by a speaker who preaches to or against someone who is not present. Underline this point in your notes and your permanent thinking: the positive, yet earnest, manner, as if explaining points to a sincere seeker after truth, should be the standard equipment with a Gospel preacher. There will be variations and some exceptions to this rule, for sometimes you may be facing an entire audience in need of severe treatment, or there may be people or a person in the audience so evil and having such influence as to justify harsh measures. But I am here simply urging you to watch the special pitfall of letting your customary spirit in the pulpit or class be that of what it sometimes has to be when we handle a special case of hypocrisy.

Here is a rule so important, that it will pay you well always to keep it in mind: people will follow the leadership of a preacher, or anyone else, who has a reputation of being careful in his talk. The Gospel preacher should guard things told to him in confidence more carefully even than the wise doctor, and watch his tongue in every relationship. Some preachers are very loose gossipers. Cultivate care at this point, and people will lean heavily upon you, knowing where they can turn to for strength. There is no substitute for that. If, in your work with a congregation, you get off to a false start with too much general talk, if you make the mistake of too much confidential talk, if you be drawn into partisanship in personal disputes, and if your pulpit and class manner of talk is of a berating spirit, you may be a wonderful preacher otherwise, but these pitfalls can easily veto all of the good that you may do. And they can become of such sore nature in a congregation as to make it advisable that you move. Why not save yourself all of that damage and trouble, to say nothing of the loss of influence for good, by paying particular attention to these pitfalls?

Approach negative issues w/ positive standpoint

CHAPTER 7
SPECIAL PITFALLS
PART 2

The "Special Pitfalls" being discussed—seventeen in all—are just what the name suggests. They are particular points of danger for the Gospel preacher. Here, as in other matters, "forewarned is forearmed."

V. Being "used."

These "special pitfalls" are not listed in the order of my conception of their importance, but if they were, I would place this one very near to the top, as to danger. Some people have use for you only when they can "use" you for their selfish interests. Once having accomplished their design, you are of no value to them, and you are accordingly dropped. As long as we live and remain human, it will be impossible to spot such characters every time they approach. Though there will never be any way to be protected entirely from them, the more we are on guard for them, the less we will be "sucked in."

    A. People will "use" a Gospel preacher often in asking questions. I mean this: they will ask questions, with no genuine intent to gain information and reform life, but simply to use the answers to "grind some axe." This often happens in classes, and especially when the preacher is new at a place, or a "situation" is in the class unknown to the preacher. Of course, truth is truth, anywhere, anytime, under any conditions. And people need the truth. But the circumstances under which a question is asked

HOW MUCH RESEARCH HAVE YOU DONE?

and answered will often destroy its value, even though the truth is given in answer. For example, here is a given class; the preacher is new to it, or unacquainted with a person in it and that person's connection with a specific problem; sister A asks a question; the question is simply designed to embarrass the person involved, and sister A is not in search of any information for herself; the truth is answered in reply, but the person involved knows the motive of sister A, whereas the preacher does not know the motive; naturally the person involved is not helped, but is incensed; the preacher later realizes that sister A simply used him to club another person in the class.

Sometimes there has been an argument in a class, or out of the class, of which the preacher is not aware.

1. One party to the argument, A, asks a question bearing on the argument, but not precisely stating the issue or correctly representing it.
2. The preacher answers the question truthfully.
3. The other party to the argument, B, makes due objection, seeking to correctly state the issue, and asks a question in the light of the real point of disagreement.
4. Brother preacher then realizes that A was seeking to "use" him to uphold A, and down B, without regard for truth.

    I have seen the same thing happen in preaching. I remember when a preacher friend of mine was engaged in a meeting where I lived. Brother or sister A sent in a written question to be answered from the pulpit. Without consulting with anyone as to what "politics" might be involved in the question, the preacher answered it. Practically all people in the audience knew that the question was involved in a long controversy which had raged in that church, in which personalities were more involved than was doctrine, and that A was simply asking that question to "get back at the other side" (he had previously ascertained where the preacher stood on the question). Naturally the answer helped no one, but fanned the flames, and gave one side a little more ammunition to shoot at the other side. To this day, I have never opened my mouth to my friend about it, though he was old enough to know better than to be "used" in that way.

Sometimes, one will ask a question in private, intending to use your answer to make an impression on others different from the actual answer you gave. The public meeting "question box" is another example of this. One factor that helped many of us to cease having such "gadgets" in our meetings was the fact that too many people asked questions just simply to have someone else clubbed. The truth can be used in such a way as to do damage instead of good. Designing inquirers can make a preacher really look silly.

B. Be duly warned of the one who would "use" you privately, while you are engaged in a meeting with that church, to carry on some grudge war. This character may really be a very good person, as to intentions, and may not be conscious of his or her "shady" methods. He—or she—often approaches you about the local elders, the preacher, or someone else. Though you do not live there and cannot know all the facts (and all the facts are difficult enough to obtain even when you live there), the inquirer tries to pull you into passing judgment on a condition or situation which should be handled by local people. He describes the case so that there can be only one answer. But the case is colored, either consciously or unconsciously. You swallow the representations, and make some move—or, at least, some comment sympathetic to the viewpoint of your informant. Later you learn that you were merely being "used." But you are quoted, and misquoted, until damage is done that cannot be repaired. Sometimes a preacher is sensible enough to see that he has been so used, but sometimes he becomes a blind partisan, incapable of correcting errors.

C. The foregoing incidents can happen with more than ordinary ease when you move to take a new job with a church. But it confronts you not merely when you go to a new location, for you will be subjected to this danger all through life. A real working on this point will certainly improve your ability to avoid this pitfall. An ignoring of its danger can so deeply involve you in this pitfall as to hasten the end of your work with a very fine church.

However, so as not to leave the wrong impression, let me mention this: this is not to advise you to "clam up" and never take a stand on anything; to be afraid to answer any question; to fear to make clear your position on any issue; or, sometimes, even as to a person. It is simply to advise caution, so as to increase accuracy of appraisal, and lessen danger at one of the most critical points of attack.

VI. "Running with" One Person or Crowd.
A. First, let us agree on this point: you may, will, and even should, have special friends.
   1. Jesus did. There were disciples in general; then, Peter, James, and John; then, John.
   2. It is a natural part of human nature to have particular friends.
   3. Failure to have such would virtually reduce a person to a refrigerator.

      Nothing that is to be said now is to be interpreted as suggesting that you cut yourself off from all close friends, thus denying yourself of some of the priceless treasures of life.
B. But, avoid three errors.
   1. Avoid being with those close friends most of the time. Constantly being with only one person or a few people in a congregation will produce four evils:
      a. Bias you in appraising conduct and needs—it being more difficult to see errors in those with whom we constantly "run."
      b. Deprive you of other associations which you need, whether you realize it or not.
      c. Deprive others of your companionship, for they need the association of the right kind of a Gospel preacher.

         Hurt your influence, as others become soured on you, figuring by your conduct that you are simply a party man and clannish. You can consider them jealous, if you wish, but you partake of their spirit in such action, so it is another case of "the pot calling the kettle black."
   2. Avoid catering to people with more money. This is observed as a common fault with some preachers, including some of our "big names." It is easy to allow people with the most money to control the policies of a congregation and the procedure of a preacher—especially if they are generous with their money in

the church and toward the preacher and his family. We who preach should remember that the apostle Paul said, "For the love of money is a root of all kinds of evil: which some reaching after have been led astray from the faith, and have pierced themselves through with many sorrows." (1 Tim. 6:10) We preach that to the church, and it is good for us to take it to ourselves. When we run only with the money crowd in a church, and formulate our patterns and actions according to their preferences, while ignoring others, we are the ones guilty of that Scripture! Some preachers just will not mention drinking—light or heavy, social or private—if their moneyed friends are given to such indulgence. The same goes for many other worldly activities—including dancing, gambling, profanity, divorcing without Bible grounds, adultery, etc.

3. On the other hand, avoid catering to people of less money. A preacher does just as much evil when he is pro-poverty as when he is pro-wealth. There is no special merit in not having considerable money or in having it, per se. To the very best of your ability, treat all people alike. Strive to be impartial. Balance your associations. It does not require much time for people to begin to say that "our preacher runs only with Brother So-and-So," or, "our preacher only runs with (fill in the blank) crowd." Someday, you will be located with a church, where only a few families or people will treat you and your family as human beings or show any inclination to be with you. You will think, then, that the advice given here is a little hard to take. I grant that circumstances will give you much latitude in applying these principles. But it still will be best for you to observe these rules, as far as all factors involved will allow. Further, you will find that, if you try to treat all impartially, you will certainly antagonize some—and sometimes those who are of influence in the church. There are people in some congregations who want special attention. They are that conceited. They think that they deserve special treatment, and that you should run after them and never make a move without consulting them. Well, there are those in the pulpits who bow to this and

"work" these egotists through that method, but it is a direct violation of James 2:1, which says, "My brethren, hold not the faith of our Lord Jesus Christ, the Lord of glory, with respect of persons." The example which James then uses to illustrate his point is simply one of many, and the principle is as broad and inclusive as there are people with whom you work. Once you start that policy, it must be kept up. And such a self-centered egotist cannot be cured by such treatment. He needs to learn that you will consider him—or her—as others, but will play no favorites. If you try to humor the person who demands it, sometimes he will turn on you, and you learn the hard way that you used the wrong and unscriptural method.

VII. Aping a Preacher

A. There is often <u>the temptation to be unnatural</u>, "preacheristic." That leads one to select some "ideal" and "ape" that preacher, copying his manner of delivery, the movement of his body, the phrasing of his sentences, his attitudes in every sermon. Sometimes this is done deliberately, but often it is an unconscious act. Men may make such impression upon you that you do not realize that you are copying them, down to the minutest details. It is easier to fall into this pitfall than you might imagine. Hence, the need for watchfulness at this point.

B. There are two very, very evil results in this pitfall.
   1. The audiences become disgusted. They will eventually catch on, even if they never saw your model. There is something almost uncanny in the ability of an audience to see through one's veneer, to see when he is simply imitating, and when he is being himself. And usually in audiences over the nation, there are people who have heard the various outstanding men among us, and they instantly detect when you are "aping" them. As your hearers are disgusted at your childishness, their respect for you is lowered, your influence accordingly wanes, and ridicule of you spreads.
   2. A second evil result is that the best in you is smothered. You do not truly and naturally develop. You are artificial, and you will never be the power that you might have been. When people call your name over the nation, the next remark will be: "He imitates

Brother So-and-So." Even if you make a good job of that imitation, you will generate more respect for yourself and create more influence if you will just be yourself. This special pitfall is very deep.

C. So, do your best to be natural. Watch yourself like a hawk at this point. If someone says, "You remind me of so-and-so," if so-and-so is a great platform speaker; nevertheless, try to change your delivery so that you will be yourself. You will be a better speaker by being yourself than by aping the greatest orator of all time. You will be sincere, and you will be you.

VIII. Women

A. Right here, in preachers' relations with women, is where some of the biggest names—in and out of the church—have tripped. It is tragic, but true. So, you might as well face it, appraise the potential dangers, and guard yourself accordingly. This pitfall becomes more "special" when we reflect upon the fact that innocent and apparently trivial beginnings can develop into evil endings. Sometimes there are designing women, who deliberately seek to lead you astray. By the same token, sometimes there are preachers of the same, vicious type, who seem to go in for that as a "career." But I am persuaded that in most cases, there are non-designing, but unwise, women—just as there are preachers of the same type. Sometimes there are women who are on the extremely silly side in public, and private—just as there are, again, preachers of the same stripe.

B. Here are a few simple rules to observe in avoiding this special pitfall.

1. As to women, be more careful with your hands than is observed in some preachers and teachers. "Abstain from every form of evil." (1 Thess. 5:22) "Appearance" of the King James Version in this text is one meaning of the Greek word, but Thayer prefers the "form"—or "kind"—here. But that will include the appearance. And Philippians 2:15 will help this point: ". . . among whom ye are seen as lights in the world."

2. Avoid being in a position with one where either of you could be tempted. Never forget 1 Cor. 10:12: "Wherefore let him that thinketh he standeth take heed lest he fall." That Scripture will help you at this point.

3. Avoid situations where the enemies could reasonably charge the possibility, or probability, of evil. After you exercise the utmost care at this point, dishonest people will seek—and sometimes find—such pretexts. And other people will believe their stories. In Rom. 12:17, the apostle Paul directed, "...Take thought for things honorable in the sight of all men." This is not the only time when Paul said that. It applies as a principle to all life—and is especially appropriate at this point.
4. Assist women with their problems, but be careful as to the how or where. One of the best things found in the New Testament on the subject of a preacher's—and especially a younger preacher, though it is applicable to all—treatment of women in the church is found in 1 Tim. 5:2, "The elder women as mothers; the younger as sisters, in all purity."
5. It is best to have your wife along, at least most of the time, in visiting women, and practically all of the time in conferences with them. If you have no wife, then enlist the assistance of some mature or aged woman, or couple. Many men have landed in this pitfall who never dreamed that it could happen to them.

VIX. Being Involved in Unwise Debates

I mean, doing the actual debating, when better judgment would dictate that more experienced and able brethren should be employed for such work. Only a few years ago, I was in a meeting with a church and stayed with a splendid young preacher and his family. They were most attractive and consecrated people. They were exceedingly friendly with me, and I appreciate them. And he had talent. He had studied the art of debating. But he had been duped into "taking on" in debate a veteran sectarian debater, who was debating our brethren before this young man was born. The young man rightfully believed that the truth of God's Word was adequate to vanquish any opponent—but he failed to understand that one must know how to use "the sword of the Spirit, which is the word of God." (Eph. 6:17) That also involved knowing something about the tricks of the opposition and how to handle a veteran, experienced opponent. He had heard the old idea that "the way to learn to debate is to start debating"—but he did not know the pitfalls of starting with an older and more able man, who was accustomed to all of "the tricks of the trade." Consequently, though he thought—he said—that he won a victory in this debate, the brethren were practically unanimous through that territory that the truth took an awful beating—not because the boy did not have the truth, but because he did not know as much about debating as he thought he did, nor did he know how the veteran opponent would maneuver. The brethren should not have carried their disappointment as far as they did, and they should have been more charitable toward the young man than they were, so far as concerned his remaining there. But brethren often are not as charitable as Christianity teaches, and in this case, they were so soured on him that they wanted him to move. They had some justification in that the young man had another debate with this sectarian booked and was determined to have it, regardless. I tried to talk to him about it, but only incensed both him and his good wife. This case illustrates this pitfall. It has happened in all too many cases and is not an isolated one, by any means. I am not advising timidity and fear, but caution, true self-appraisement (Rom. 12:16), counsel with and consideration for the brethren, and extreme slowness in arranging debates.

CHAPTER 8
SPECIAL PITFALLS
PART 3

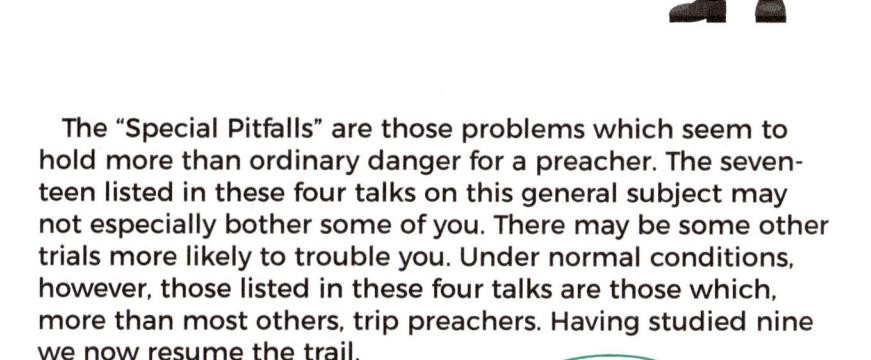

The "Special Pitfalls" are those problems which seem to hold more than ordinary danger for a preacher. The seventeen listed in these four talks on this general subject may not especially bother some of you. There may be some other trials more likely to trouble you. Under normal conditions, however, those listed in these four talks are those which, more than most others, trip preachers. Having studied nine we now resume the trail.

X. Going to Seed in Crusading for One Issue.
  A. First, so that we will not be misunderstood, let us make three points as clear as crystal.
   1. Local conditions determine the emphasis in preaching, though we are to preach only the truth, and all of the truth. Never is there to be any deviation from the truth of the Gospel. (2 Tim. 4:1-2) But points to be stressed will be decided by conditions in a given place.
   2. Men on the ground, including the preacher, usually know more about local conditions and needs than does someone who lives elsewhere.
   3. The preacher is to stand, without wavering, for the right and against the wrong. He has to be constructive and destructive, for and against. This is proved in the two following Scripture citations in the teachings of Christ. As to being "constructive," or "positive," as

brethren so often advocate, in preaching, our Lord taught that in John 18:37, "To this end have I been born, and to this end am I come into the world, that I should bear witness unto the truth." Brethren say, "Preach the truth; give us positive preaching." So did Christ in that Scripture. But brethren often say, "Don't be negative; don't condemn; don't oppose; don't specify false doctrine; just tell the people what the truth is and do not single out error for specific mention or identification." Here they contradict Christ's procedure and orders, for in Matt. 16:5-12, there is the story of our Lord telling the disciples, "Take heed and beware of the leaven of the Pharisees and Sadducees." They thought that He referred to bread, but finally there dawned upon them the realization "that He bade them not beware of the leaven of bread, but of the teaching of the Pharisees and Sadducees." He specified both the doctrine and the religious party teaching it. His "beware" certainly put this teaching in the negative, destructive, condemnatory class. When brethren today rule out that kind of preaching, they take issue with the Master Teacher, Jesus Christ, in favor of much of the modern teaching and preaching spirit. You take your choice, but I prefer to stand with Christ. I am saying all of this so as not to be misunderstood in what follows. Nothing that I shall now say is to be construed as contrary to these three points.

B. But, it is possible to "wear out" an issue, even though one is on the right side of that issue. For example:
1. We may "harp" on some evil, and carry it to the point where people get tired of hearing that. If the preacher persists in that theme, the people then become disgusted.
2. That, in turn, will do more harm than good. People who might otherwise be won to the right side of the controversy, or whose opposition to the right side might be neutralized or held to a minimum, may be driven into the camp of the enemy. True, they should see that truth is truth, regardless of how much a speaker stays on one subject. But taking people as they should be and as they are cannot be confused or considered as the same status. We have to recognize how the human mind operates, and act in accor-

dance with known human procedures. The sum total of "the truth" is large enough to enable us to have some variety in our preaching, and to allow room for much emphasis upon specific evils, without going to the extreme of staying on a point until people who are not as solid as they might be are repelled in disgust.

C. Now, let me use four specific examples.
1. Millennialism. I teach that current millennialism is a heresy, and oppose it as such. It contradicts the Gospel of Christ in all of its principal features, and in most of its minor ones. Further, I teach that those teaching the doctrine, and calling themselves members of the church, should be corrected and converted; that, if they persist in their false doctrine, they should finally be disfellowshipped. Since these lectures are not being devoted to a discussion of such points, but rather to the mechanics of doing the work of a Gospel preacher, I shall not stop now to give Scriptures for this attitude. But my attitude toward this issue is stated, so that you may fully understand how the millennial issue is used as an example of "going to seed" in crusading on a given issue. If anyone wants my reasons for thus opposing millennialism, I will be glad to supply you the Scriptures and also let you have a tract I have written and circulated for years on "Certain Scriptures Contradicted by Premillennialism."

On the other hand, suppose I stay on that subject, and that is about all I preach for months and will not let it rest. People would get tired, and finally disgusted. Why? They would want a more balanced diet. If that be true in the human body, it is true in preaching. "Let not then your good be evil spoken of." (Rom. 14:16) Of course, some evil people will speak evil because they seek for pretexts. But the appeal is not to put a club into their hands, or to unnecessarily make the wrong impression upon others.

2. Some local point of worldliness. For example, I teach against the modern dance, that it is sinful. I intend not to ignore it either in "holding a meeting," or in engaging in full-time work with a congregation. Those who want nothing said about that issue,

then, would not want me for either type of preaching work. It is my conviction that it should be often noticed in our preaching. That is because of the great drift among us toward worldliness, because of the increasing pressure of worldliness from the outside, and because the modern dance is a growing menace. So many well-known preachers among us will hold meetings and will either say nothing or little about this evil, or they will select some morning crowd to preach against it, when only a comparatively small percentage of the congregation is present, practically no outsiders, and with all the young people in school. Some of them are tearing up the church over other issues, some of which are purely imaginary, and "fiddling while Rome burns" in ignoring worldliness in general and the modern dance, social drinking, and "light" gambling in particular. They pride themselves on "keeping the church sound," but are really destroying the soundness by being indifferent to the cancer of worldliness that is eating at the very vitals of the church.

However, just as in the case of millennialism, I could go to an extreme in preaching against any type, or all types, of worldliness. If I never let the subject rest, and "harp" on it continuously, the same pitfall occurs. Sometimes men had to leave churches where they preached. It was told that they left because the churches "could not stand preaching against worldliness." The truth was that the preachers stayed on the subject and acted as if no other subject was worthy of being considered. They simply wore the people out on a subject that could have had much preaching, but good was defeated by poor judgment as to frequency of preaching on worldliness.

3. Taking up paper agitations. Sometimes that becomes a fever, or even a contagion. Men think that they have to line up, count noses, and get on the bandwagon. Now, I recognize that most of our religious papers do much good. Being operated by human beings, they all do some harm, for human beings are not guaranteed against mistakes. A very few do so much harm that the brotherhood would be blessed if they were buried and forgotten. But the

most of them do so much good that we are blessed by them. We should not discount their influence. We should consider their positions, and stand with them for things that are right and against things that are wrong. Generally they are trying to help the cause of Christ. If occasionally you find one that must have issues in controversy to survive, and could not endure without such issues, don't judge all of our Gospel journals by such measure.

When all of the foregoing is said, however, it still remains true that, if you are not very careful, you can find yourself waging the personal grudge battles of a paper in your preaching, with the same evil results. Some of these "crusaders" give every sign of crusading as a sham or cover, while actually carrying on a personal war. Instead of being made a "sap" by such an outfit, as some of us have been, steer clear of such as you would avoid the leprosy. If such an outfit writes you up, it will not hurt you in the long run, but will be to your credit. You do not have to line up with such an outfit to prove your soundness. Even after you exercise the utmost diligence at this point, there will be times when you realize that you are "sucked in." The best encouragement I can offer you is that, if you will watch this phase of your work with the greatest care, you will fall into this special pitfall less often than if you are indifferent to its dangers. I am thinking right this minute of a good man, of high motives, a good speaker, who would have split a church if he had stayed another six months, just because he became wedded to the idea that a certain paper was the sole hope of keeping the church sound, and he "followed the party line" of that paper on every issue. He thought—and thinks—that he was fighting for Christ. In fact, he went to seed on crusading for issues, deceived by a paper's agitation, and almost split a fine church. He will ruin his best usefulness in the church if he doesn't "come to himself."

4. Carrying your local church problems—and disappointments—over from one place to another. This is one of the easiest traps in which to fall. Perhaps you have had severe problems or trials at a given place of residence. They have been extraordinary, more press-

ing than many other troubles. Perhaps you have been deeply disappointed in certain brethren in their failure to stand up and support the truth, and you, in a crisis or under pressure. You experienced some of the apostle Paul's "in perils among false brethren." (2 Cor. 11:26) You left that place, whether in defeat or victory over those evil forces, with scars branded on your heart because of fickle men, who would allow you to lead in cleaning up some dirt, and who would then show no real and sincere appreciation. I am purposely drawing the picture rather darkly for the sake of impression. Your experiences may have been similar to these, either worse or not so bad. But you had these problems. Then, you moved to another work. Right here is a special pitfall. Leave the problems, the "disciples of the cross and double cross," and the disappointments of that place behind, and do not carry on the wars of that location in the next job. It is a good rule, in the first place, when you are an "ex-" to be an "ex-." Some preachers, even after they leave a work, keep on meddling with it. Where you are now is a new work. Yes, I know that human nature is the same everywhere and the same problems in principle will be in every place. But there will be variations. And, if you handle the new job like you did the former one, you will be making a mistake, for jobs are different, as children are different. If you carry your old troubles into the new work and keep waging those wars, you will find resentment, a hardening of heart, and soon a one-way ticket out. And if you don't get that one-way ticket out, you still will do needless damage, little good, and will be treating unfairly the people in the new work.

D. This business of going to seed for one particular point of truth, at the expense of neglecting other needed truth, and to the disgust even of those who stand with you on principles of right, is one of the "most special" of these special pitfalls. It seems one of the easiest mistakes to make. Oppose error, but try to keep a sensible balance. As difficult as this is, make it your lifetime business, and it will help you to grow in effectiveness, plus cutting to a minimum the damage you will do in being deceived at this point of danger.

XI. Length of Sermons.

Remember the old quip: "A sermon to be immortal, need not be eternal." Another one is: "If you forget the hour, keep up with the day of the week."

  A. In determining the length of sermons, there are many factors involved. Here are at least some of them.
1. There is the ability of the speaker. Some men, therefore, have the ability to interest audiences in longer speeches than do others. However, pure, unadulterated conceit sometimes enters the picture right here. Men impose upon audiences because of that conceit, knowing that they have this power, and presuming to abuse it.
2. Sometimes there is the special character of a sermon or an occasion. Upon such special occasions, people usually are prepared for longer sermons, covering more ground and giving more data on an issue.
3. Then, there are the types of service which normally vary. I mean, for example, a Sunday night service can normally take a slightly longer sermon than the morning service. With considerably more people usually present Sunday morning, more time is nearly always required to complete a service. With less time customarily required Sunday night, that provides a little more time for the night sermon. However, sometimes circumstances will change this. Too, the night service of a "protracted" meeting will ordinarily allow a longer sermon than Sunday morning—though young people in school are due more consideration at this point than they often receive.
4. Then, sometimes there are special needs, peculiar to a given time.

These four factors will forbid us attempting to make any ironclad rule as to the length of sermons. And I certainly do not set myself—or any other man—up as an authority for regulating the length of all sermons.

  B. But some observable signs can help us at this point.
1. People today hear more preaching than was true when most of the old-timers among us were young preachers. Many years ago, because of the scarcity of preachers and infrequency of sermons, people naturally craved more preaching, with longer sermons. They would have to go great distances for the com-

paratively few sermons they heard. Of course, they then would be willing to listen to two-hour sermons, and want more when finally the speaker ground to a stop. Now, however, in the average place in this country, preaching is many times more frequent, and even regular. They can hear preaching almost any time they wish—both in assemblies and on radio and television, and also in so much access to printed sermons in magazines, papers, books, and tracts. The men who make it a practice to preach in meetings for an hour, and often longer, and who do little better as to length in the regular Lord's Day service, seem to forget this difference in conditions now and some years past.

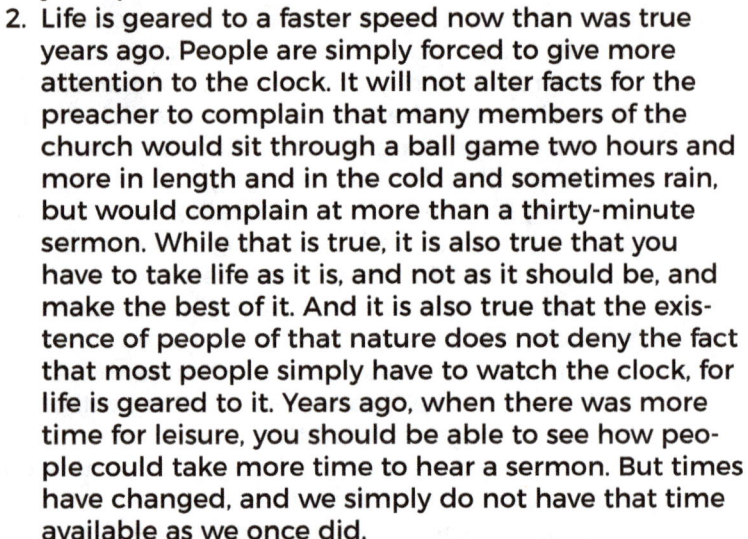

2. Life is geared to a faster speed now than was true years ago. People are simply forced to give more attention to the clock. It will not alter facts for the preacher to complain that many members of the church would sit through a ball game two hours and more in length and in the cold and sometimes rain, but would complain at more than a thirty-minute sermon. While that is true, it is also true that you have to take life as it is, and not as it should be, and make the best of it. And it is also true that the existence of people of that nature does not deny the fact that most people simply have to watch the clock, for life is geared to it. Years ago, when there was more time for leisure, you should be able to see how people could take more time to hear a sermon. But times have changed, and we simply do not have that time available as we once did.

3. Habitually long sermons have at least four evils.
   a. They wear people down. "Blind" preachers have trouble seeing this, but it is a fact. I have sat in services when people all around me were restless, tired, and grumbling because the preacher didn't stop, and he went on, blissfully unaware that his audience was sore.
   b. They hurt the attendance. It is true that sometimes men of extraordinary ability draw good crowds in spite of their long sermons. Sometimes the crowds are due to the loyalty of the disciples, or special interest in the occasion, as much as

— START OUT W/A BANG → AND QUIT ALL OVER —

being due to the speaker's ability and reputation. What this blind preacher doesn't realize is that he would have even better attendance if he would use some discretion.

(c.) Habitually long sermons <u>damage the good that the speaker might otherwise do</u>. It is another case of allowing "your good to be evil spoken of." A man might preach the truth all night, but, if he continues on and on to the point of audience-exhaustion and to the disgust of people, he has created ill will and made the people unfit to consider fairly the good that he has preached. ▶ *THINK MORE THAN OTHERS...*

(d) These sermons <u>usually betray</u> conceit. We concede that sometimes it is a case of a speaker being so interested in his subject that he loses all track of time. But more often, it is due to egotism. The proof of that is seen in the way such speakers defend their long sermons when reproved, the way they talk about how people formerly loved long sermons, and how they compare the way people will take a long ball game with the length of a sermon they desire. Such defense shows that the preacher thinks people should be willing to go to any length and trouble to listen to him until he is ready to stop. He may point to his crowds, the number of calls he receives for meetings, and the big churches that invite him. Grant all of that, young men, and we will say that such a preacher is in error and doing the church and himself some damage. He could have all of those good things of which he brags and by which he defends himself in an even greater degree, if he would cut down to a sensible length of time. He is "getting away with it" now, but doesn't realize that as he gets older, people will say, "Don't send for old Brother So-and-So because he will preach all night." Because others betray a high degree of conceit at this point is no reason why you should fall victim to this vicious evil.

ARROGANCE OR SELFISHNESS

It does appear that this error of lengthened sermons grows worse, at least with a majority of preachers, with age. Some young men, we concede, are chief offenders. And some more mature and aged men grow into the practice of preaching shorter sermons. But, as a rule, this long-sermon complex seems to fasten itself more upon men as they become more mature and aged. You can see how this could easily happen. The older men grow in ability to preach the more they have learned, because of the accumulated years of study and filing information in their minds and among their notes. They are better prepared to present a greater variety of information to their audiences, and in a more interesting way. "That figures." But there also is the danger. Often a man's greatest strength becomes his greatest weakness. Hence, let us draw two conclusions about this special pitfall:

a. Be careful of this danger in your first days of preaching.
b. As time passes, years fly by, and your wealth of material accumulates, plus your increased ability to present your information in an interesting way, be increasingly careful of this danger. I am not here recommending the twenty-minute sermonette. But you can lay to this: the habitually long sermon is as inevitably a pitfall to a preacher as is death certain to all men. You should not be encouraged to ignore these hard, cold facts just because you know some able preachers, in demand over the brotherhood, who are "long-winded." They will run their course, and find their calls dwindling, if they do not change. After all, you may pile on one or two hours of data and sermon points, and people may be duly impressed with your information and platform ability, but they will not retain all of that mass of information. Why not hold yourself to thirty minutes—except upon very special occasions, and sometimes less, and stand more chance of the people retaining and digesting what you have given them? I have lived and preached long enough to be able to call the names, were I disposed to do so, of some great men, good characters, and able preachers—as well as some of the

other kind—who spent their last days in limited preaching because of their reputation for wearing people out in sermons. Beware of this special pitfall.

XII. Fads.

Sometimes a preacher becomes obsessed with some fad, and makes a hobby of it. Or, he may pick up some practice that is not necessarily a fad, but he makes a fad of it. That will detract, disgust, and damage. It is easy to drop into this pitfall, especially if there is a wave of this particular fad sweeping the country, or if some very splendid man in whom you have great confidence has taken out after it. Let me cite you two practices as examples.

  A. There is the case of catchy phrases. They may be true, and proper—or they may not. But, remember this: even if they be true, they can be repeated so often as to get tiresome and lose their benefit. Sometimes, when we first hear them, we repeat them, because they sound attractive. Even if there be some truth in them, but when carried to the end of the line, their ultimate conclusion, they may become untrue and damaging in their implications and effect. An example is the denominational saying, "As goes the Sunday school, so goes the church." Just think through that catchy saying, instead of thinking about it. Consider the implications. Now, I push the Bible school "like nobody's business," as we sometimes say. I teach that members are in duty bound to attend and bring their families. And it customarily grows. But I do not even believe that "as goes the Bible school, so goes the church." When there are so many important features having a bearing upon the future of the church, it is a pretty large order to say where the main emphasis is. This phrase puts too much emphasis upon the Bible school and sidetracks some other very, very important influences in the church's life. For example, could you not, at least with some reasonableness, say, "As goes the eldership, so goes the church"? Isn't it true that the leadership of God's people has always determined its direction and progress? Since the elders are the overseers, or bishops, of the church (Acts 20:17, 28; 1 Pet. 5:1-4), the pastors (Eph. 4:11), doesn't it follow that the policies and procedures of a church will be set by the type of eldership of said church? Again, could we say, "As goes the pulpit, so goes the church"? Isn't it true that the preaching poured into a church all of the time will determine the character of that church? And isn't it true that a very weak eldership sometimes forces a pulpit to wield greater power and force in order to save the church from a weak and divided eldership? Or, vice versa? Could we not say, "As go the homes, so goes the church"? Really, isn't the home the basis of human training and character? Doesn't it set the pattern more than any other one agency—at least, in the early and formative years? Then, when we say, "As goes the Bible school, so goes the church," we can very easily exalt that above other equally important influences, even above the home—when, really, the home has so much to do with the number and character of the Bible school attendants. The danger here, then, is, first, in saying something that is not necessarily true; and second, in sidetracking other profoundly important agencies; and third, in so riding this fad as to be unable to see anything else, even exalting it above the assembly worship of the church—which is precisely what the denominational bodies have done. That can either make a church of Christ partake of the spirit of a sectarian body, or so sour more sober and sound brethren on you as to cause you to learn "the hard way" just how much of a special pitfall this is. The elements of truth contained in this saying can be stressed properly without adopting that as a slogan with all of its evil and denominational implications. But we hear something like that; it sounds true and seems good to help us to make a point; someone whom we admire says it; and we start it as a sort of a fad without thinking to the end of the line.

Another example of these catchy phrases is this, or some variation of it, "A man does not have to get seasick to do missionary work." For years I have often heard and seen that remark in print. It invariably comes from one who is, at least indirectly, making light of evangelism in foreign countries. The expression sounds "cute" to some people, and usually evokes a laugh—generally from those who stand against foreign evangelism. If you corner the one making that remark, he will not actually say that he is against churches sending men to foreign countries to preach the Gospel. There are too many

Scriptures which such a character would have to openly defy, and he is afraid of that. But somewhere along the line, he obtained an objection to this type of work and began to make light of it. There have been abuses and actual wrongs done in this field of church endeavor, which I have also opposed. But the abuse does not justify us in spending our lives slurring the need for and practice of supporting Gospel preachers in foreign countries. They talk about "heathens in this country." Right they are—and they will be here as long as time lasts. They talk about evangelizing our own state. Right again—but the Great Commission (Mark 16:15-16; Luke 24:47-49; Matt. 28:18-20) did not direct us to spread out to "all nations" only after our own country had been evangelized. Many peoples have never heard the Gospel and do not have the chance that America has to hear. So, think several times before you use this slurring, catchy phrase, for it will reveal a heart in actual opposition to the Great Commission of Christ, a narrowness incompatible with Christianity, will put your influence squarely against congregations supporting the truth in foreign countries, and will promote selfishness. Sooner or later, all of that will bear evil fruit in your life, and you will again learn how a "cute" and catchy phrase can be a very special pitfall for a man who is supposed to be a preacher of the Gospel of Christ.

B. There is the fad of "sex education." Just as much of the world around us in America has gone to seed and slush on this, so have some of our own people. Waves move over the country. They affect the church. The very nature of this subject, young men, makes it:
1. Dangerous as to propriety.
2. More in the realm of family responsibility—though I am not denying that preaching along principles involving this has its place in a Gospel pulpit.
3. More out of place in teaching to mixed classes.
4. Especially out of bounds for young preachers—and the older preachers should take care at this point.
   Boiled down, this fad, which is now spilling into our ranks, can easily become something that is coarse and revolting. People will come to look with suspicion upon the thinking of those who go in for much of this. Many colleges in this country, operated by

people of the world, are almost lewd in their courses in "sex education." It has always seemed so easy for some of our people to take up anything the world uses. Some of our men—and women—writers get this in universities and books. Then they rush into print with some of this "stuff" that is downright lewd, suggestive, and unfit for publication. They have apparently swallowed the worldly idea of holding back practically nothing along this line. The world is harping on the fact that children and young people formerly were not adequately prepared for these problems, because the families and teaching circles played "hush-hush" with such subjects. Even if we grant that the pendulum swung to that extreme, we have certainly observed that when some of our paper writers, preachers, and teachers start to correct that deficiency, they go to a most lurid extreme in the other direction. Just why is it, brethren, that when we start in to "ape" the world, we "out-ape" it every time? And right at this point, some of our teachers and writers are distinguishing themselves for having absorbed an extra measure of this in the places where they have studied, and they will in time, if not careful, make the sex education of the world read and sound like a very tame brand of teaching compared with what "we" are doing. Please watch it, and don't swallow this evil, or take for granted that to teach just anything along this line is "O. K." This is one place in our present program where I fear we are getting downright silly—plus being on the filthy side. In your preaching and teaching, keep your eye on this special pitfall.

XIII. Fatal Disappointment Over Defeat of a Cherished Project

A. What often happens is this: a preacher becomes so interested in one project, <u>that he values the entire worth of his work by that project alone</u>. He seems to forget everything else, and he gives all of his attention to it. He goes to work to win the congregation to it. It may fall flat, starting with the elders—and that is the place usually for it to start! But the church cannot be won to the project, and it falls flat. Then the preacher is so deeply disappointed that he is ready to leave. I grant that such a

situation could happen to any preacher, and with good point. But this happens too often, when it is so unnecessary.
B. Ordinarily there are five errors in this situation.
1. <u>The preacher may value that project too highly</u>—though obviously it would be impossible to convince him of that fact. Sometimes a detached view, some years later, will bring him around to that way of thinking.
2. <u>He certainly is far too impatient</u>. A Christian, in general, should not be that impatient, and especially should a preacher learn to have more patience. If it fails to go over, he can let it rest awhile, and perhaps try it again later, or try another approach.
3. <u>He gets out of humor, and shows it.</u> That does not help any situation—in business, in the home, among friends, or in the work of the church.
4. <u>He so antagonizes others as to lose his influence over them forever.</u>
5. <u>He is so disappointed as to be forever unhappy there.</u> Even if he does not show his being out of humor, but feels this way about it, he is making the same mistakes in attitude and procedure. You have to learn to take defeat and keep at the work. You will find that this special pitfall is especially adapted to young preachers—but it draws into its smothering grasp those of all ages. Old ones in years sometimes never grow up in spirit. There is no need to be such a big baby that you "get mad and go home," that you "pick up your marbles and will not play," when you can't get your way about something. I have known men to leave places in such a petulant spirit, just because of this special pitfall, when their leaving was senseless and all uncalled for. And sometimes, they have been forced to leave because they acted so childishly when their cherished project failed.

CHAPTER 9
SPECIAL PITFALLS
PART 4

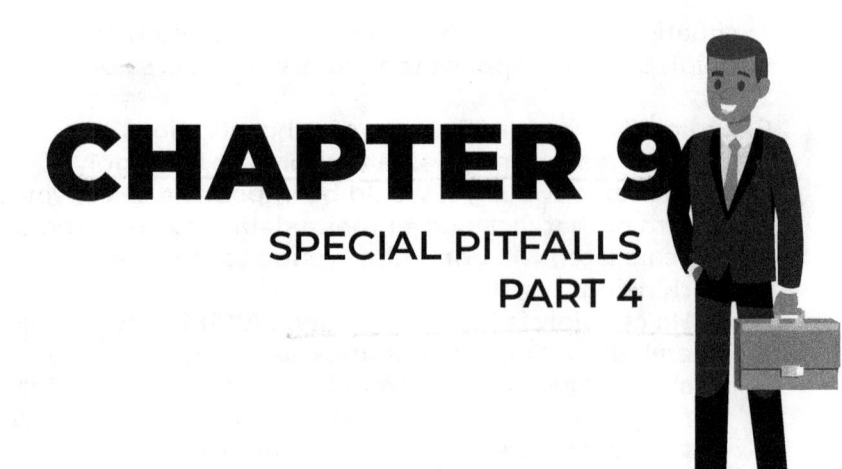

The seventeen "special pitfalls" being discussed in these classes have been selected, from among the many dangerous areas for a Gospel preacher, as among the most potent threats to the success of his work. They have been carefully screened. They are among what many preachers consider as "little" things. But they have tripped many evangelists, and among the number, some of the very best of men. On the other hand, do not allow them to influence you to shrink from the challenging and soul-saving work of a preacher of the Gospel of Christ. Prepare yourself to steer clear of these pitfalls, and courageously move forward. "We walk by faith" (2 Cor. 5:7) should be a rule which preachers should demonstrate as efficiently as they urge it. Now, let us examine the last four in this series of seventeen.

XIV. Your Length of Stay at a Place.
  A. There are too many factors involved in this problem to permit an ironclad rule for all places, or even for you to plan to stay at any one place a definite number of years. But in this, as well as in many other of our problems, we are pursuing two objectives:
   1. Dealing with your general attitude toward this problem.
   2. Pointing out some clear pitfalls to avoid.
  B. There are at least four basic pitfalls of attitude to avoid.

1. Avoid having a definite length of time in mind. One of the most absurd ideas is this: "Three years is long enough to stay at one place." The circumstances of your work determine the length of your stay. Each place is a separate one, with different conditions. At each place the preacher performs differently, usually learning by experience and improving with each change of location. (From the many times some of them change locations, then, they should show remarkable improvement!) A preacher should naturally improve in efficiency. The accumulating years and his growing familiarity with the job where he is would enforce that idea. If he is not growing, then many Scriptures are nullified and violated, such as Heb. 5:12; 2 Pet. 3:18; Eph. 2:21; Jude 20; 1 Pet. 2:2. Who would be so impractical as to think that there would be spiritual growth without improvement in the use of talents and general efficiency? Mark this down and forget it not: if a preacher thinks that a set number of years on a given job is his limit, usually that conception alone will stifle, smother, and prevent growth. Men—and women—do not make such arbitrary rules as to how long they should stay on a job in secular professions and trades. Then, why should such absurd notions apply to how long preachers should stay on a job? The idea probably originated from the Methodist plan of more or less regularly shifting their preachers around, and we are great, sometimes, on "aping" the world. But even the Methodists are veering away from that and allowing more and more of their clergymen, through petition of their congregations to the higher authorities, to stay longer in given localities. If they are learning, it seems that we could do the same! Three years might be a proper length of time to stay at a given location, three times three years, or three minutes. Or, three years might be three years and one day too long! Just as the local conditions and circumstances of your work will bear upon that question, sometimes the circumstances of another offer, with your future in mind, will properly bear upon the question. As a rule, two or three years will so introduce you to your work that then you will be just ready to render your most effective service.

On this point, we can easily flop from one extreme to another. We can see a preacher who stays far too long at a place, and we can go to the extreme of barely getting started before leaving. Oh, we can know of some preachers and churches who are noted for the two-year tenure, and we then go to the extreme of over-staying. This definite "term of office" idea is a pitfall, regardless of the precise number of years you plan to stay.

2. Avoid the extreme notion of "if one is against me, I will leave." The enmity of one may be a compliment, and to leave in the face of such opposition might weaken the church and strengthen the spirit of compromise. Many good preachers have left jobs because some evil peanut opposed them, and both they and the church lived to regret the flight. A church can thus be turned over to Satan, and the task of a preacher and the sound element of a church will be made more difficult when a preacher does come along who is not to be bluffed.

3. On the other hand, steer clear of the extreme of "they can't run me off." That can become the spirit of stubbornness and factionalism. It can do untold damage to a church. Such preachers have caused many church divisions, unhealed for years or generations. There is a line to be drawn between unflinching courage and standing by your guns in the face of evil, and that of stubbornly setting your face to stay at a place at all costs. Sometimes it is difficult, apparently, to distinguish between justifiable standing pat and plain stubbornness. Watch your heart and make sure that your unyielding courage does not become personal aim to have one's way, just to "show them that they can't run me off."

4. Avoid taking a job just long enough to get something better financially. The preacher is not honest who says within himself, "I will take this job just until I can do better elsewhere financially, but I will not tell the church that." Now, I am not necessarily opposing your taking a job with higher pay. But if your policy is simply to use a church until you can "do better," that will damage you in character, in all of your attitudes, and in influence. I concede that there could be a sit-

APPS - BUSINESS EXPENSE

uation where you might accept work with a church, at insufficient support and such employment to last only until you could obtain sufficient support elsewhere—but that should only be with the full knowledge of the church, and by mutual agreement.

But in the final analysis, let your usefulness be the determining factor in the length of your stay at a place—and let that be decided by you and the elders, or the responsible leaders of the church if there are no elders, rather than by a vote of the congregation, as engineered by the preacher. The church may decide that your usefulness there is at an end, whereas you may think it is just beginning. You may be correct, but if the church decides that your usefulness is at an end, it is, for you could not serve the church against the wishes of that body. It still "takes two to make a trade." This is why I say, let your usefulness be decided by you and the church, and not just by you. Getting into a war over how long you should stay at a place is definitely a special pitfall to watch.

XV. Working Too Far Off From the Elders and Deacons.
A. The proper order is for elders, deacons, and preachers to work together closely, as a team. The elders are the overseers, or bishops. (Acts 20:17, 28) They are the shepherds (1 Pet. 5:1-4), or pastors (Eph. 4:11). They are spoken of collectively as "the presbytery," (1 Tim. 4:14) suggesting their working together as a unit, or body. The same unity which should characterize their working together should be true of the way they, the deacons, and preacher pull together. The preacher is employed by the elders, and he is under their oversight, just as are all other members. With all of the elders usually employed in secular work, and unable to give full time to the church, they usually look to the preacher for much executive work. In a business enterprise, if an executive official and board of directors do not work closely together, the business will be damaged in many ways. While the parallel between a secular company with its directors and executives and the church with its elders and preachers is not a perfect one, there is enough parallel between the two situations to make the "illustration illustrate." Deacons are assistants to the elders. They have their separate office, as in 1 Tim. 3, but they have no separate authority, as do the

[Handwritten margin note: Preach for the Cause, not for Applause]

elders, and are under the elders' oversight the same as all members.

→ The church looks to elders, deacons, and preacher for their respective functions. Divisions within that leadership team will necessarily trickle down into the membership in general. If you cannot or will not work closely with the elders, you are headed for trouble. If you pursue that as a policy, and intend to build your life along that line of procedure, you would do better to quit preaching—and fast.

B. Sometimes a preacher tries to work aloof from the elders, and sometimes an elder is cold and inhuman toward the preacher. Men working together should exercise a personal interest in each other. There should not be fear, suspicion, or envy. A preacher needs to seek the counsel and companionship of the elders. The elders need to take the same attitude toward the preacher. Neither is sufficient to himself. Neither can say to the other, "I have no need of you." If either thinks that, it is a case of unmitigated conceit, proving the one guilty too little for his position in the church. Such preachers and elders uniformly cause trouble, either guiding the church into paths of error or holding the church back—or both. Neither preachers nor elders should be glorified refrigerators, living in a shell, sublimely ignorant of how each needs the other, and inflated with an egotistical feeling of his importance and self-sufficiency. May the God of heaven help us to have more big men, and fewer peanuts, in the pulpit, in the eldership, and in the deaconship.

C. Someday you may unfortunately find yourself in a situation where you feel the necessity of helping the church to clean out a corrupt portion of its leadership. Pray God that such will not be your lot. As a rule, if that has to be done, it should be left to men of more maturity and seasoning. Sometimes we hear of some "smart" young preacher—and sometimes we hear of some who are not so young—going into a church and early starting at the business of cracking at the eldership. If you find yourself in a situation as a young man where such reform is needed, it is generally best to go elsewhere and leave that to older men, letting the church handle its own affairs. Many of our older men feel that it is always best to leave such a situation to the congregation to "sweat it out," on the ground that, if a church has neither the conviction nor the courage to eliminate a corrupt or disqualified leadership, it does not deserve anything else. I do not entirely subscribe to that idea, for occasionally you will run into a situation where your sense of honor, decency, and loyalty will not allow you to run. In that case, you have to prayerfully make up your own mind.

One concession I should make, in fairness to you, so that you may consider all of the angles, is this: the men who urge that you should always ease out of a situation meriting a cleanup, and never become involved, will correctly urge that practically all churches will accept your help in such a crisis and praise you to the skies for standing your ground and helping to overthrow the forces of evil; then, when the battle is won, they will show little or no appreciation, and they will give the material rewards to those who had no part in their struggle and victory. Many a preacher has helped the righteous part of a church to clean up the church, place it on a sound basis, so that the church has then grown and flourished; then left; then the very ones who were most benefitted in the church will close the door to the one who helped make their position possible—aided and abetted by some political opportunist of a preacher who made no sacrifice to make the recovery of the church possible, but who uses the recovery to feather his own nest. Certainly, young men, that will be the final chapter in most cases, and those of us with some years of experience behind us know that to be true. For that reason, the average preacher of age refuses to help a church in such an emergency because they know that many of those who praise him the most when they need him will turn against him when they do not need him. So, they figure, why throw yourself away for people like that?

Still, my counsel to you would be to do your duty as you see it; take life as it comes; don't get an idea that it is up to you to save the church alone; don't get the "crusader complex"; but don't run from the clear call of duty; know that if you lead a church out of the swamp of stagnant filth on to high and dry ground, you have done the cause of Christ a service, regardless of what rewards you obtain in this life; leave the rewards to God in eternity, and don't worry! If you feel the need for comfort and friendship of people, know that you have that, often when you least expect it, and that a few grateful people are worth many times more than the other kind. After all, your own self-respect must be kept in view. Probably the best thing to do is this: take warnings on both sides of this question, and then figure your course of action in line with what you conceive to be the clear call of duty. And always lean heavily upon the arm of prayer.

XVI. Financial Debt.
A. Financial debt seems to be one of the most devastating plagues to preachers, and for at least four reasons.
   1. It is sometimes difficult to draw the line between sincere but poor management on the one hand, and willful indifference to bills on the other. Sometimes we are too quick to judge a man to be deliberately dishonest with his bills, when actually he is more irresponsible as a manager. But poor management can certainly sink your financial boat.
   2. The exacting demands of the public also make it easy to contract too much debt. People in the world—and in the church—have many expert ways to help preachers spend their money!
   3. The training and natural desire of a preacher to be liberal with his money in the Lord's work combine to make financial debt "just around the corner." He spends more time with the Bible than do other members, by the very nature of his work. He studies in a very special way the Bible teaching on the subject of Christians being liberal with their money to the Lord through His church. Their average contributions, as compared with incomes, will run far, far ahead of practically all members. Occasionally, you find a preacher who contributes "lightly" to the church. Generally they contribute more than anyone else, considering incomes. And they spend money for the Lord's work far more than members know, or can know. So, their money just naturally gets away from them more quickly than that of the average member of the church. And that in spite of the fact that he knows he does not have the "company" provisions and benefits had by most people working with great companies—and he usually has to pay all of his social

security tax alone, with no help from his "company," as employees of worldly companies have. But his very liberality is also a danger, in a sense. Surely be liberal—but more careful because of that.
    4. Nothing will so completely destroy a preacher's influence as will debt. For some peculiar reason, the public will more quickly forgive affairs with women than financial debt. Right or wrong, deserved or not, there is no escape from this fact, and you might as well face the reality. There is no way to avoid it. The purest character and ablest platform man can have his influence either ruined or tragically impaired by debt and financial ruin.
B. In view of the damage that this "special pitfall" does, let us notice some warning signs.
    1. There is the ease with which debt can be contracted in these days. That is true of all people, and it is especially easy for preachers, in view of public interest and confidence in preachers.
    2. There is the possibility of taking a job at insufficient pay, because of a desire to help a church in need. If this happens, you had best either get your income increased at that job, or change jobs.
    3. There is the sign of that poor management. Sometimes this means living beyond our salary in getting what you want, regardless of prior obligations. If you are in debt and barely getting by, it would be both foolish and downright dishonest to buy something that you did not have to have, just because you or your family craved it, and place yourself where you could not pay bills. When you are in debt, young men, the most important thing for you to do with your income is to live as frugally as possible, pay your obligations, and wait to buy something that you can get along without until you can do so and honorably take care of bills. If you can't deny yourself to that extent, you need a guardian and the church needs another preacher! Always attend to your smallest bill with scrupulous attention to details. Never let a bill come due, if you find yourself unable to pay it, without having made arrangements with your creditor—and before the due date.
    4. There is the warning sign applicable to all true

preachers of the Gospel: we are thinking more of spiritual matters than material ones. That is where our mind is. We are absorbed in all details connected with the work of winning souls to Christ and keeping them with Him. But this business of keeping straight with the world financially is one of the "details" involved in our work. Getting hopelessly involved in debt will ruin your influence in spiritual matters and place you where you cannot influence souls to Christ. Anything that nullifies or damages your influence is of necessity a most important matter.

XVII. Handling of Controversial Matters.

This is one of the most "ticklish" of these pitfalls. Because people, including preachers, allow their emotions to upset them so easily in dealing with points of disagreement, this is really a major one of the special pitfalls. Let me suggest three principles to guide you through this field of danger.

A. In the first place, be certain of your convictions. Have those convictions, and be true to them. That will necessitate considerable study of God's Word, for it is the standard by which we are to be judged. (John 12:48) Once establishing to the best of your ability what God's Word says should be your conviction, then make up your mind, "having done all, to stand." (Eph. 6:13)

B. In the second place, respect the convictions of others. Multitudes of other people are sincere and intelligent, even if there are many others who are neither. It is not a mark of soundness to preach in the attitude that all who disagree are either dumb or insincere. One of the best known preachers in the Old South is a man who has made a deep imprint on the hearts of many people. To them he is virtually a god, though they do not realize it, for they accept his word without question, to the point of rare fanaticism. It was formerly my conviction that he had done far more good than almost anyone in the whole brotherhood whom we might name. But the years piled up evidence that I had allowed myself to be made a fool in so thinking, acting, and defending him, and I sadly learned that he had done far more harm than good. I formerly thought that he was largely responsible for the growth of the church in that great area, and made some foolish comments, publically and privately, to that effect. But I finally learned what many of his followers will never learn: that the progress of the church in that area was in spite of and not because of him. In addition to riding many hurtful hobbies through the years, he simply will not respect the convictions of others, growing worse about this as he grows older. In fact, he preaches, argues, and writes as if they have no convictions if they disagree with him. His hateful sarcasm is the worst I have ever known, and he has vetoed much good that he might have done by consistently taking the position that all who disagree with him are either dumb or not sincere, and are seeking the popular side. Yet he wants all opponents to believe that he is strictly honest and knows what he is talking about. This is a tragic trait of character to cultivate.

C. In the third place, do not fear to tell your convictions, "... for we cannot but speak the things which we saw and heard." (Acts 4:20) The preacher who maintains a policy of never making known his stand on controverted points is an unsafe teacher. When the church's position becomes jeopardized by a challenge of error, he would not lead the people into righteousness, but would follow the crowd. As when Israel, in Exodus 32, introduced the calf worship, he would follow the example of Aaron in going along with the crowd, rather than that of Moses in standing firm and breaking up the apostasy. Beware of the preacher whose stand on any question you cannot ascertain. I am thinking of a younger preacher, of several years' experience, in a city where the orphan home and Herald of Truth issues are live. We have had difficulty learning the position of this brother. Finally, another brother pinned him down to a direct statement, and he said this: "There are good arguments on both sides and wrongs on both sides. I have friends on both sides, and I do not want to say anything that would antagonize people and interfere with my preaching the Gospel." Needless to say, he has no convictions; or, if any, they are so weak that he fears to take a stand. He is trying to stand in with all sides, agreeing with whatever crowd he is with. If all were like him, the antiorphan home, etc., people would take over a town and he would do nothing to stop it. Try his position with the anti-Bible class people, the millennialists, the missionary society folks, and the instrumental music in worship people, and see what happens to the church. He will reap the benefits of the church being saved by the radical extremists, but will do nothing to help bring the benefits. Such people belong to the family of Pilate—"willing to content the multitude." (Mk. 15:15) Of course, you don't have to make a pest of yourself, and become generally obnoxious. As much harm can be done in going to one extreme as the other. But just make certain that you courteously, in love, but firmly make your convictions known as it becomes sensible to do so. With the political opportunist, there is never a sensible time to express convictions in the face of possible opposition.

Let me illustrate the application of these principles with a specific problem—handling the carnal warfare question. I do not hesitate to say that my understanding of the New Testament is this: a Christian cannot kill for anyone, under any circumstances. Who will deny these three propositions? In fact, the third one is a necessary conclusion from the first two.

1. The spirit of carnal warfare is that of hate. I doubt if anyone in America would deny that, though some insist that they have gone through war without hating. I would accept their word, but insist that such would be exceedingly difficult, and urge that the proposition is true. Armies proclaim that to be a good soldier a man must be a good hater. All training is slanted to make a soldier hate the enemy.
2. The spirit of Christianity is NOT that of hate. (1 John 3:15; Matt. 5:43-47) By hate in each proposition, we refer to hatred toward people. The first Scripture in proposition two even makes it clear that the hater cannot spend eternity in heaven.
3. Well, if the spirit of war is the spirit of hate, and the spirit of Christianity is not that of hate, the third proposition is a necessary conclusion: the spirit of war and the spirit of Christianity are hopelessly irreconcilable.

    Further, there is nothing in the New Testament to indicate that a Christian operating in two realms is not responsible for what he has to do in the realm of human government. A Christian is always responsible for every act, and there is not one line in the New Testament to suggest that he can ever pass the responsibility for his act from himself to another person or to some unit of society. (Rom. 14:12; 2 Cor. 5:10) He is also to obey the civil law as long as it does not interfere with Divine law. (Rom. 13:1-7; Eph. 1:22-23; Matt. 6:33; Acts 5:29) Nowhere does the New Testament even hint that I lose my personal responsibility when I am following the orders of civil authorities. Now, in handling this question, apply the three rules I suggested, and let come what may.

D. I am not conscious of having preached regularly at any place where I did not apply these three principles on this question, of knowing my convictions, holding to those convictions, expressing those convictions. But extra care should be taken in the handling of all such questions. On many points of deep controversy among our brethren, it must be remembered that emotions are supercharged. That is especially true in the war question, where patriotism to country has, in a majority of places, dethroned prior obedience to Christ, and where many intemperate parents are more bent on defending what their sons and daughters have done than they are in upholding what Christ has authorized. They decide what they want to be true, and then try to make the Bible prove their desire. Equilibrium seems harder to retain in such matters. Hence, let us remember that slower progress will yield greater ultimate dividends. A young man makes a tragic mistake in beginning his work with a congregation by immediately jumping into such questions. He had best get himself firmly established first; do such teaching on any question that is necessary, of course, but remember that age, experience, and seasoning will help him to retain his soundness, while at the same time handling such questions with care and methodical progress. Just remember this: you do not have to get the church straight on all controversial questions in the first thirty-six hours after you hit town. You can destroy your usefulness in a place by too much haste and too little restraint.

Now, let me ask you to review the list of seventeen "special pitfalls" given in these last four lectures. I do not suggest or even imply that these seventeen points are the most important ones in all your preaching career. But this is a selected list of problems which seem to me to have been the most dangerous of all I have known and heard of, in all my acquaintance with preachers, in tripping preachers and destroying their effectiveness at a given locality, and, sometimes, in all the brotherhood and throughout their lives. While others should doubtless be on the list, I believe this: he who successfully handles these seventeen dangers will be able to handle any others without very much to worry about. "Wherefore let him that thinketh he standeth take heed lest he fall." (1 Cor. 10:12)

CHAPTER 10
THE PROBLEM OF VISITING

In this lecture we are confining ourselves to the personal visiting by the preacher and his wife. The question of developing a visiting program, participated in by all members of the congregation, will be discussed in the next study. The importance of this subject justifies our allowing it to consume a whole period.

I. **An Extremely Wide Difference of Opinion as to Methods.**

Let us be fair, and admit in the very outset that there is by no means unanimous agreement among preachers as to this work of a preacher's visiting, and/or that of his wife's. Perhaps we will find more difference of judgment in this than in any other field of a preacher's work. That fact, instead of discouraging us, should spur us to a more intensive study and search for the best methods.

A. One extreme view is this: preachers do little visiting, and take less responsibility for influencing others to do it. They reason that this is the church's duty. Some become more specific, and say that this is the elders' obligation. I heard one preacher say, "If the elders don't give me something to do, I'll go fishing." Then he smirked as if he had said something cute. The elders should have given him something to do—to move out of town. I do not mean to imply that there is anything wrong with a preacher spending time—much time—in fishing. There is intended no criticism of that. But the point is this: a preacher should be able to find something to do, even if the elders have no specific tasks or suggestions for him. It is right and proper for preachers to be willing to receive counsel and suggestions from elders, and for elders to assume some responsibility as shepherds in so doing—without being mere foremen or lords! (1 Pet. 5:1-3) But it is definitely out of bounds for a preacher to do nothing until the elders map out something for him. He has a responsibility for personal visitation among the congregation and outsiders, and he should not take the extreme view that such is altogether the church's duty and no part—or little—of his. Some other preachers reason that they will spend practically all of their time in study. Now, study is an absolute necessity for a preacher, and we made that quite clear in a previous lecture. But study without liberal visiting among the people can be—rather, is—evil in its deficiencies. Such a course robs a preacher of something he desperately needs—the human touch. He needs to associate with people beyond the time when he sees them in church services and classes. He needs to be with all of the people of a congregation, and not just with his friends. The more he comes in contact with more people, the closer he becomes to their lives, problems, needs, and the better he can translate his studying into applying the principles to the needs of the average man. He who buries himself in his study and visits little or none may become a scholar, but he will also be impractical, visionary, aloof, and unacquainted with the people to whom he is trying to minister.

B. Another extreme is this: the preacher "stays on the run" all of the time, visiting, to the plain neglect of his study and of his home life. We admire his zeal, but do not recommend his judgment. Those who are, by his visiting, influenced to attend church services do not hear anything worth listening to when they attend, for the poor fellow is so busy with visiting that he spends little or no time in study.

C. There is a happy—and necessary—medium.
   1. As to the first extreme, we agree:
      a. The church is under obligation to do this type of work. We are to follow the example of Christ (1 Pet. 2:21) in seeking and saving the lost. (Lk. 19:10) We

are to "have the same care one for another" (1 Cor. 12:25) in the church. So, certainly, in those principles we have a clear mandate to go to people, to seek them out, to come into personal contact with them, whether in or out of the church. That will necessitate personal visiting.
   b. The preacher is not employed to do the work of the members—including the elders. Each one must do his own work, to the extent of his or her ability. (Rom. 14:12; Matt. 25:15) No person can do another's work. The preacher is employed to assist the church, but not to substitute for it.
   c. If the preacher does not major on study, those who are influenced by his visiting to attend services and classes will receive too light a diet when they attend.
2. As to the second extreme, we agree:
   a. A preacher can certainly overdo the matter of visiting, thereby becoming unbalanced in his work.
   b. He may neglect study and home in his incessant visiting, day and night; whereas, both study and home have their just and definite claims.
   c. Members can be pampered and spoiled by such a preacher. They can come to expect so much attention beyond what is reasonable, proper, and necessary. They will become permanent problems and will forever vex elders and later preachers who have a more sensible and balanced conception of the work.
   d. This builds a congregation with false conceptions of individual responsibility and work, with tragically false conceptions of the proper work of a Gospel preacher and his relation to the church. A church built upon false conceptions will cease to be a New Testament church. This all gives ammunition to the radicals who seize upon such isolated cases and falsely accuse the whole church of turning over the congregation to mere "preacher-pastors."
3. But, when we say all of the foregoing, we still insist that the preacher should do visiting that is considerable as to amount, that is steady and planned. He will exert a definite influence on the person visited. Even if the one visited never responds and forever

stays away from Christ and the church, there will be an indirect influence upon those who are connected with the one visited. Often this indirect benefit or influence will spring up in quarters of which one does not even dream. His personal contacts influence the general feeling over the community. His personal visiting gradually fixes him in the public mind as interested enough in people to take some time with them. There is simply no substitute for this visiting.

Perhaps you are thinking of some "big name" preacher among us who has the reputation of doing none of this. Well, show me that "successful" preacher who has done little visiting over the congregation and community, and I will show you that same preacher as being tremendously more successful if he would supplement good pulpit work with more visiting. I have seen both sides of this question. I came out of college with my nose turned up at this work of visiting, saying, "I don't want to be a modern pastor, all the time running after people and nursing them." Well, young brethren, I can say that I have not changed my conviction along that line. I still do not want to be and to do that, but the recommendations which I am here making to you about visiting represents the convictions which have become gradually fixed through years of actual work. You can engage in much personal visiting, and still avoid the evils of "the modern pastor system." I am willing to lay these "middle-of-the-road" suggestions by those of the two extremes mentioned in this talk, and you take your choice.

D. Right here let me say just a brief word as to methods.
  1. They will naturally vary with places, conditions, ability, and experience.
  2. So, we now pass to some recommended principles and plans, to help with working out specific methods. Here again opinions vary. Here I wish I had time for a whole series of talks on this subject, for I have tried to make it a "major" in my work, without losing sight of other essentials and without losing my balance.

II. The Preacher's Personal Visiting.

Keep in mind this is largely a matter of planning and orga-

nization. That will make the real execution so much easier.
  A. First, let us lay down this principle: the preacher, in his visiting, should major on five types of visits. They should be:
    1. Sick and shut-ins.
    2. New members.
    3. Weak (spiritually) members.
    4. Aged people.
    5. Prospects—for baptism, for restoration, for placing membership.

    There will be many other visits, of course. But through the years, your principal emphasis should be on these categories.

    Please let me add a section here as to why I name the foregoing five classes as those upon which to place major stress in visiting. The sick and shut-ins easily and naturally commend themselves to us. "I was sick and ye visited me." (Matt. 25:36) Sickness is a time when people usually need special encouragement and fortification against loneliness and/or discouragement. Occasionally I hear of a preacher saying, "If you are sick, send for a doctor." Right then, the elders should send for another preacher, if this brother can't be taught more of the spirit of human kindness and desire to take a personal interest in the ills of the people. And habitual, long-time shut-ins especially need that sunlight of human interest. They naturally look to a preacher for such. He is employed full time in the work, and has more time than many other members for visiting. His study of the Bible should more deeply impress him with the multitude of teaching in the Bible on the subject of ministering to the sick—and visits of friendliness and encouragement surely constitute a part of effective ministering, even though there are other ways also to serve them.

    New members deserve a friendly welcome into the congregation. Some of them can easily adjust and adapt themselves, while others cannot. But all of them need the outstretched hand of fellowship—not confined to greeting at the church building, but reaching into their homes and associations otherwise. Where I labor, I habitually urge the members to immediately start visiting new members. Because of the number of members, sometimes of new members, and the fact that the preacher is one man, the others will often—or sometimes—get to the new members before the preacher. But it should not be much ahead of him. He should practice what he preaches in this, as well as in everything. Spiritually weak members certainly are entitled to special attention. The parables of the lost sheep and the lost coin, (Luke 15:1-10) plus many other Scriptures, teach this. Why should the preacher not here again set the example, by the very nature of the case? Aged people often receive less attention, are in their twilight days, are often more sensitive, and are deeply grateful for help. Besides, we can learn much from them. Prospects for Christ and the church naturally are in line with our work, interests, and duty. They should not be high-pressured, but definitely, persistently, wisely, lovingly sought.

B. Let us now move into some points of procedure.
1. Have specific reasons for that visit, hoping to accomplish definite objectives. It may be only to "soften" that person, preparing for later and more serious discussion—but do what you are there for. Don't do visiting just to be killing time, or so that you can say you have made so many calls.
2. Let the purpose of the visit have much to do with the length of it. Too brief a "pop call" will sometimes put a bad taste in one's mouth, and it is equally true of a visit that is prolonged beyond all reason and sense, to the wearing out of the patience and disgust of the one visited. If you see that you are not accomplishing your purpose, or having great difficulty doing so, it is nearly always better to terminate the visit as gracefully as possible, and try it again later. Especially is this to be remembered when visiting one who is sick, or trying to teach one the error of his ways, or visiting one who seems indifferent to your visits.
3. Often take your wife. Propriety will demand this in many cases. In addition to being absolutely necessary at some places or situations where you visit, it is also true that your effectiveness is greatly increased if she can and will do considerable visiting. Of course, the church should not be encouraged to feel that it

has employed your wife. She has her normal life to lead, with the same duties of house and family which others have. Under normal conditions, she will be the busiest woman in the congregation. So, I am not recommending that you place unnecessary burdens upon her, and kill her early with unreasonable demands of time. No job is ever worth that much or that necessary, and never is that right. But we can say all of that and still hold to the conviction expressed: that, considering abilities, your wife can be a great help in this work.

4. Soon after you begin work with a congregation, I would urgently recommend this: you and your wife begin a plan of visiting every family in the congregation. The aim is: to familiarize yourself with the families of the church. Make those visits fairly short, except in a few necessary cases. You can't just move on clock schedule, but have to yield one way or the other in some instances. I know that you may object to this, arguing, as I did early in my work, that "it is the duty of the members to visit us first, for they were here before we were, and common, ordinary, decent manners would demand that they so do." Well, you can save some of the more snooty ones till the last, and spend not much time with them. Meanwhile, some of the better ones will show an interest in you and your family. But, in spite of what people should do being so different from what many of them do, I still urge that you follow this plan.

This move will have these advantages, in addition to the overall aim I suggested:

a. It will establish you in a better position as to the good will of the church.
b. It will generally serve as a good tonic for the church.
c. Without being too "nosey," you will learn much about the church that you would otherwise require much longer to discover.
d. It will prepare the ground for later, more extended, more direct visiting with enlarged and specific purposes.
e. This is, therefore, a basic visiting program, for the early part of your work with a given congregation.

5. Keep records of your visits. As to the type and extent of records, certainly I would advise against too much detail. It is much better to have fewer details and look after them properly, than to weigh yourself down with too much of this. You can learn by trial and error as you move along what records are the most valuable and practical to keep. But, above all, make them and keep them.

   Records of each visit, whether in home, hospital, office, or anywhere, will help you to keep up with the progress of your visiting. They will assist you in not overlooking people that should be visited. They will enable you to answer, with dates, persons, and places, those who unjustly criticize you for lack of attention to themselves or to others. These records will spread information before your continual attention which will be useful in your working with different people. You will find this point especially helpful in dealing with prospects. By all means keep a prospect file—a simple card index of people who visit your services, or who may not have attended, and who may be considered prospects. On one side of the card, have spaces for their name, address, telephone, and when attended. On the other side, have space for the worker—yourself or someone else—who visited them, needed remarks, and any vital information you deem pertinent. Brief, but pointed, notes will chart the progress of your work with that prospect. Often look back over these cards and study different cards with a view to planning the next move on that prospect. And remember this: the more you study the science of making records of your visits, the more compact but useful you will learn to make them.

6. Just a word about "problem cases." They are unreasonable time-takers and attention-demanders. You will have them in almost any congregation, and especially is that true as you deal with larger churches. (However, they are not such big pests in larger congregations as in smaller ones. The smaller the church, the more a problem case sticks out like a sore thumb). In dealing with these adult babies, keep three rules in mind.

   a. After you establish beyond any doubt that they are

that type, devote just enough attention to them so as to prevent any sincere person being made to believe that you took no interest in them. You could come to the point where it would be best to entirely ignore such pests.

b. But do not allow them to take up much of your time. If you "pet" such characters, you will have to do it as long as you are there, in order to retain their good will. That will disgust sensible members, and can vault that spoiled member into a position to do real harm. It is no more right to humor babyish members of the church than it is to humor children and spoil them in your family. To do so will have the same effects in both cases. You have so much more important work to do than to waste your time in trying to humor spoiled members of the church—regardless of who they are, to whom they may be related, and how much money or influence they might have.

c. Do not engage in a lot of worrying about such problem cases. They will usually fall of their own weight. That is even true of those who have a dominant influence—elders or wives of elders. If your failure to "pet" them means the loss of your job, you have your self-respect, and in the long run, you gain even in this world, to say nothing of the world to come.

7. Seek to learn the best time to visit people, and, as nearly as possible, do your visiting at that time. I know that the preacher has a busy schedule and sometimes finds it almost impossible to reconcile the multitude of forces pulling on him with the convenience of the one being visited. But the more you visit one, especially a prospect, at a time inconvenient for the one visited, the more danger of irritating and alienating the one in whom you are interested. It is not difficult to learn the habits of people, and you can often fit yourself into their schedules without much trouble.

8. Always keep personal cards, to leave in case you visit an address and find the person gone. Your visit has not been in vain, for he or she knows thereby that you have been. If you have no cards, you can still let

the person know of your attempted visit, but you will find the card a distinct asset. Make the card simple, instead of cheapening it by a veritable mass of Scripture quotations and other data.

9. Never allow yourself to become discouraged about your general visiting program. Sometimes you will come to see that you must abandon all further efforts to influence a given character, and you sadly and reluctantly scratch that person off your list. But, even so, sometimes you will try him or her again. Then you may learn that the attitude has changed, and you make progress with speed. The very visiting which you previously did, and which you deemed a failure, may be responsible for the progress that you now make. Even if you abandon one for life, you still should not become discouraged. If you fail with one, you succeed with another. And there is no way of estimating how much good you do, year in and year out, in visiting and working with people. If you seem to have more trouble than do some other preachers in influencing those whom you visit, remember that the Lord doesn't judge you by another's ability, but by your ability, and will hold you responsible for doing only what you can do. If you seem to have difficulty in influencing those people, keep studying and trying, and you will make progress. Two books which will help you with this problem are Brother Otis Gatewood's You Can Do Personal Work, and Brother Homer Hailey's Let's Go Fishing For Men. But the more you study them, the Bible, and life, the more you will realize that methods must be adapted to separate cases, and that the longer you go in life, the more you will learn about how this should be done. And never lose sight of this: the more you visit and work with people, the more you help them and yourself.

CHAPTER 11
DEVELOPING THE CHURCH IN WORK PART 1

We next spend a major portion of our time in studying how we may train and develop a church as workers. We will deal with the "brass tacks" of how it is done, and urge specific features in our work that should be stressed.

I. Influencing the Church to Visit.

By "visiting," I have references to visits to people, in or out of the church, that have definite objectives in mind, objectives that pertain to the saving of the soul of the one visited. These visits are in the nature of calls made upon people with a view to influencing the ones visited to bring their lives more in line with the wishes of God and Christ. Just as an insurance agent obtains the name of a prospect and goes to that house to talk with the person about buying insurance, I am thinking of these visits which are made on specific people for particular purposes.

A. Make it your business to train that church to be a visiting congregation—regardless of its size or location. The basic principle and justification for this point is stated in 1 Cor. 12:25: "...but that the members should have the same care one for another." In that chapter, from verse 12 to the end of the chapter, the apostle Paul is showing the parallel between the human body and the spiritual body, the church. It is stressed that in the spiritual body, as in the physical body, the members feel the sorrows and joys of each other. The implication is, then, that they show an interest in each other by serving one another. That necessitates going to the homes, offices, etc., on visits with definite purposes. But the principle of taking an interest in people is applied in that Scripture to the church. Then, connect it with Luke 19:10, teaching that Jesus came "to seek and to save the lost," and 1 Pet. 2:21, teaching that we are to "follow His steps." That will be sufficient evidence to establish the principle of taking interest in those out of the church. When, therefore, you train a church to be a visiting church, along the lines of these Scriptures, you are leading that church into the path of putting said Scriptures into practice, instead of merely preaching about them.

Not only do the foregoing Scriptures justify this work, but actual experience reinforces the command by showing real results. For example, we have found in years of trial and error that, if people will be influenced by the preacher contacting them, they will be influenced by any and all Christians visiting them. They are not surprised, usually, when a preacher calls, but seem to be amazed when others come to them. They are surprised that others have and will take the time to search them out and spend time with them. Obviously, the more people doing this work, the greater the influence. Theorize all you wish about this being someone else's responsibility; when all is said and done, your pushing this work will mean more to the influence of that church, and of yourself, than can ever be put into words.

B. Let me now suggest some specific methods. Of course, it goes without saying that different men will use various methods. Any plan that I or anyone else would suggest would have to be adapted to your own ideas. But the following simple methods have been found to be effective in my own work, and will probably be helpful, with your preferred modifications, in your promoting of visiting by the church.

   1. Collect and maintain a list of those needing visits. That list can be collected from these sources:
      a. Those who visit the church services where you labor—signers of guest books or cards, and those whose names you can obtain who may not sign in such a way.
      b. New members—and they certainly rate special attention.
      c. The sick and shut-ins.

d. The spiritually weak.
e. Members apparently having little social contacts with other members—some guidance here going far toward helping the timid to become adjusted.
f. Prospects for baptism, for restoration, and for placing membership with the congregation.
g. Miscellaneous, whose names are gathered from various sources and for different reasons. One thing to keep your eye on is this: when members learn that you are making a serious effort to build a list of those needing visits, some members will load you with names just to satisfy their whims or flatter their vanity in saying that, "I gave brother preacher a name to visit." The judgment of many people is poor, in the first place. And they will often give you a name to be visited, when a visit from any member of the church would do more harm than good. You will have to learn about this in "the hard way," but a caution now and extra care on your part will save waste of energy and embarrassment later. Beware of the member who is simply afflicted with "I-want-this-name-visited" complex.

2. Keep a prospect file. Now, a list of people needing visits, as just discussed, would contain probably most of those in the prospect file, but would also have certain members of the church who, obviously, would not be on this prospect file list. I mention that so you will not confuse the two. This prospect file is a separate feature of your work in equipping yourself to promote visits by the members of the congregation. In this prospect file, keep just enough data on every card to make your file simple, workable, practical, and up to date. You can smother yourself with details and data that would require an office force to keep. The longer you go, learn to streamline the details, stripping to barest essentials—and then keep up with the information.
3. Assign visits. You can do that in classes, before and after church services, or whenever you come in contact with those you wish to do the visiting. Let me give you one example of how I make these assignments. In my work with the Homewood, Bir-

mingham, church, I have a Bible class on Tuesday mornings during the fall, winter, and spring. I make many of these assignments in that class. Sometimes I give the card assignments to the people—women, and a few men attend—as I meet them coming to the class. Sometimes I call them out to the class and ask for volunteers to take the cards. If volunteers lag, I give the assignment to someone. It is best to use both methods, for that furnishes variety. We not only give names of people to be visited, but some to whom to write notes. Out-of-town visitors, and some from the city, are sent notes of appreciation for their visits to our services. We do not send them printed forms, but each one receives a personal note written by some member of the class. Sometimes we substitute a telephone call of appreciation. In all events, the task is assigned, and no one is missed. The reason that assignment is insisted upon is this: many members say that they do not know what visits to make, but will make a visit if you tell them one to visit and the reason for the same. While some do not need that guidance, but have enough initiative to search out people to be visited, it is still true that many lack that ability. They will accept a definite assignment and glory in the specific task.

4. Use cards for the assignments. Get standard, 3x5 cards, writing name, address, and telephone number of the one you wish visited, together with the explanation as to why you wish that visit made. The carded information serves as a more definite guide.
5. The worker should know what he or she is expected to accomplish. Be sure that the worker is fully informed as to the type of visit to make in each case. A worker making a visit, with a hazy idea as to why the visit is being made, is liable to make matters worse for the one contacted and for the Gospel. Sometimes it is difficult enough when the worker has a clear idea as to what the object of the visit is. How much more confusing and likely to failure is that one where the worker has not been adequately "briefed!"
6. To fully inform the worker as to the object of the visit, you will have to carefully appraise the one to be visited. The more time you spend in studying that which

is to be accomplished in that visit, the less likely will you send the worker off on a "wild-goose" chase, with more harm done than good.
7. Insist upon the return of the cards—signed by the worker who made the contact; dated as to when the contact was made; giving a report of the visit, telephone call, or note written, with any data that the worker feels that the preacher needs. This serves many useful purposes.
   a. It, first, impresses the members with the fact that something definite is being done in having that "care" for people.
   b. It establishes responsibility.
   c. It gives a record of the reporter, in case—as often happens with me—you want some point on the card report clarified, or want additional information about the one visited.
   d. It saves a lot of talk that would be necessary if that worker gave you a report simply by word of mouth.
   e. It files that information for future reference.
8. Have follow-up visits. That is vital. Study the people to be visited, and the reports on the back of the workers' cards. See that the follow-up visits are wisely spaced and that the one visited is not unduly "rushed." However, sometimes there will be need for great concentration of visits. That will depend upon the case and will be more cause for study on your part. Even after you exercise the utmost care, there will be mistakes as to the frequency of the visits. But it is better to make mistakes doing something and trying, than to make the mistake of doing nothing because of the fear of making a mistake.
9. Have good tracts available. Keep workers informed as to what tracts are available. Occasionally, give instruction as to how to use them. Since I am devoting a larger section to tracts later, I will leave the subject now. But it is certainly not debatable that if you engineer and promote considerable purposeful visiting by the members of the church, there will be many times when they can effectively leave good tracts on their visits.
10. Frequently talk to the church in general, and to

smaller workers' meetings in particular, as to how to do this work. You will find that, if you will push this feature of your labor with a church, there will be more visiting done as a result of the assignments you give; these same workers will do more additional visiting "on their own" as a result of the stimulation you give in their assignments; other members will catch the contagion and do some visiting that they would not otherwise have done; the congregation will have a better spirit and will develop a growing interest in people. While other preachers will, in some cases, turn up their noses at this program, you will go right along your way building congregations and helping people to have a new appreciation of Luke 19:10 and 1 Cor. 12:25.

II. **Training Classes.**

We shall discuss three types of training classes. Of course, almost any class could qualify as training, and would have that result, even if there were other principal aims. But the three types of classes we shall now study are essentially in the field of training.

A. First, let us consider the public speaking class. I believe that herein is one of the most profitable methods in developing a church in work. You may be reluctant to try this in your early years, reasoning that you should wait for more maturity and experience before attempting such a program. Don't wait. You can make a success of it, even in your first years. You can study the question. And you have an advantage, in that most of the members have not had as much training as you have had, nor as much experience. To have such a class will mean much to the church in the years to come, in general leadership development, and in the making of elders, deacons, teachers, and preachers.

For many years, I have been conducting a class in public speaking of this type. One night per week is devoted to it, with the season usually running eight months, and having a summer recess. Some recommend shorter seasons. No ironclad rule can be applied to that question, but the length of time devoted to a season should vary with circumstances. The people of each community would be the best judge of that. Each session runs a little under one and one-half hours. The class moves on strict schedule, with one man keeping time. The bell stops a speech or class discussion of a man's performance at the time designated—and the bell means "stop," not "just a few more words." The ideal program consists of four who read passages of Scripture, of 15 verses each; 3 minutes class discussion of how the readers performed after each reading; one book report of 10 minutes, giving a report on some portion of a textbook in public speaking or sermonizing; a 5-minute class discussion of both the reporter's report and the content, divided about 2 and 3 minutes respectively; three religious talks of 10 minutes each; a 5-minute discussion by the class of each speech following each assignment.

We are using a tape recorder. Each entire program is recorded and left on tape for many weeks, giving the men time to come to the building and listen to themselves. Not many will do that, but a few will, and it is worth doing if only one will take that much interest in his own improvement. Someone should work the tape recorder who knows how to do it, and who will not kill so much as 30 seconds in time. And this program involves some money invested in several rolls of tape. But the benefits more than justify the expense.

If you use a tape recorder in this type of a class, you may find it necessary to shorten the program here suggested, to avoid dragging it out too long. In that case, I would advise one less speech. You could have the three oral readings from the Bible, the one book report, and two religious talks, with suggested discussion after each one. Or, if you find it impossible or impractical to have the book report, you could omit it and have three religious talks with the Bible readings.

In playing back the program, we usually play back a little (about one minute) of each man's part. Though you do not get the complete picture of his performance, you get a sample, and by playing back a part of each man's part, you play no favorites and no one is disappointed that he was not heard—by himself and others. You may prefer to concentrate on one or two men each night and take more time with each playback, but rotate among the men through the weeks. Absenteeism may make that more difficult. You can play each man back each night, consuming one minute on the playback, take that off of the discussion period, and avoid lengthening your program any. Three things I know: almost any program is better than no program; you can vary this suggested schedule to suit yourself; the tape recorder will do so much for your class—as well as being useful in other ways in the church—that you will be astonished at the results.

This program affords instruction and practice in oral reading of the Bible; instruction from some recognized authority's textbook in speaking and/or preaching; practice in religious talks; the benefits to the performers coming from class criticism; the benefits to the class of active participation in the criticisms. I lead the discussion with enough speed to prevent languishing and dragging, and the class will always inject enough humor to avoid any undue embarrassment. We do not "pull punches" on anyone, and stress in public announcements that one should not enroll in the class unless he can take a real "taking apart"—and "putting back together." The whole program, with roll call and necessary announcements, will consume close to one hour and 30 minutes. Assignments are made weeks in advance, especially the book reports and talks. The church owns four copies of the book for the book reports, and thereby each man has at least three weeks to prepare his report. We have one alternate reader, an alternate book reporter, and one alternate speaker, to stand by and step in, in case someone on the program is absent. The absent man then gives his part the next week, in place of the alternate. The book reporter does not prepare two assignments, but gives the one he would have regularly given if he had not been forced to substitute. Then, the man for whom he "pinch-hit" gives his own assignment on the following week. In that way, there is seldom a hole in the program.

Now, the foregoing is a standard program, but should be varied at times. The program opens and closes with prayer, and it is understood that anyone, including novices, may be called on without notice to lead one of those prayers. We do not criticize or practice the prayers, but instruction in leading prayers may be given at intervals. Once or twice a year we have "open night," inviting any and all, including women, to attend. Especially do we always have that "open night" at the last class of a season. I doubt the value of having women spectators during the regular season.

This type of class can be adapted in any of its features to any place or length class desired. You may not care for the type program I have described, though I have used it, with a few modifications, for years, and with sustained interest and rarely a dull moment. But the point is, any plan is better than none. If you prefer an entirely different plan, use it. If a man will really study this work, he can conduct almost any type of class with profit. It will be up to the instructor to use his own preference. But a class of this type will do amazing things for the men and young men, for the church in developing leaders, and for the general feeling of the church. The men even love purely a men's class, with only the males of the species present! Why don't you try it? A church does not grow too large or find itself too small to be benefitted by this class. A church that will carry this kind of a class on through the years will never find itself short on material for elders, deacons, and teachers among the men, or those to do anything in the public work and worship of the church. The churches that you find drying up and lacking these men are those who make no efforts along this line.

B. Next, there are special teaching courses that will be of immense help in developing the church in work. During the past several years these courses have gained in great popularity among churches of Christ. My conviction is that they should become an annual, or at least a frequent, part of the program of a congregation.

  1. The purpose of such a course is to improve the present teaching force, and to train and develop additional teachers. How could anyone discount or deny the value of such an endeavor, in view of the absolute necessity of people accepting God's Word if they are to be saved, in view of the fact that the church is the only institution on earth for the teaching of that holy Word, and in view of the truth that all individuals in the church are accountable to God for doing as much of the work as possible? That, then, involves the use and improvement of our talents.
  2. These special teaching programs can be accomplished in various ways.

  a. You can give intensive study to the subject, and at intervals give some instruction on the subject of teaching.
  b. You can have a short course of a few days, with someone or a group especially qualified to give that instruction.
  c. You can bring in individual specialists at different times, with said specialist instructing the teachers in that particular age or grade group.
  d. If a church is not financially able to bring in several teachers at one time, be it remembered that any time you bring in a qualified instructor for the entire teaching force or for any one teaching classification, for a week, five days, or one day, that time and money are not wasted, but will contribute to the sum total of the progress of teaching efficiency in that church. Where the congregations are near enough to our Christian colleges, they can often have some of the instructors for single sessions, without excessive inconvenience or monetary cost.
3. I agree that much of this which is done today is impractical and useless. Just because someone is announced as a "specialist" does not make him or her that. You had better do some extensive checking before you swallow some of that propaganda. But that can be done. Because some are taking advantage of a proper trend and abusing the confidence of the churches, does not commend our judgment in going to the other extreme of losing all benefits from some of the useful work that is being done. And the trend to place emphasis upon these special teaching courses, in improving the quality of our teaching, will certainly grow. Among churches of Christ today, there are more people who are making a special study in the field of training the congregations and individuals in better teaching, and who are assuredly qualified to be of great help in that work. After you thoroughly investigate the people available for this work, and after you discount the froth and high pressure along with the impractical and visionary, you will nevertheless find many able "specialists" among men and women who are qualified to give

expert instruction in their fields to those interested, and within scriptural limitations—women teaching women and not women teaching men, according to New Testament limitation. Our colleges, papers, and preachers can give you some guidance in selecting the proper ones, if you need that help. We do have the material, and it is growing by the year—both in number and quality.

C. A third feature of our training classes should be more emphasis upon singing schools. Many, many years ago, much work along this line was done. Consequently, people knew more about the rudiments of music, and the singing was much more accurate as to notes, correct as to tempo, and leaders who knew their job were many times more abundant than now. Congregations knew more songs, could more quickly "catch on" to new songs, and probably sang with more zest. All of that was the natural result of the members generally being more familiar with the principles of singing and having song leaders who knew what they were doing, musically, and who stood before congregations confident that their leaders knew what they were doing. The reverse of that general familiarity with music and musically-efficient leaders would of necessity produce lack of confidence, fear, and reserve in singing. Then there was a decline in interest in this work. We shall not attempt to fix the blame for that, for probably no one today knows the precise cause of this decline. One thing we generally agree on: the number of men capable of teaching profitable singing schools is low indeed. They are scarce, though there are some good ones. I believe that perhaps we are seeing some signs of at least a moderate revival of interest in this work. May God speed its return.

A regular, special course in the rudiments of music would be helpful to any congregation. If annual courses could not be arranged, at least an occasional one would help. With the very proper opposition we make to mechanical instrumentation in worship, we should place a corresponding emphasis upon instructing our people as to how to sing. We should not be content to oppose the innovations and evil in such worship, but also instruct in how to do properly that which we do not wish to be polluted with "the doctrines and commandments of men." Such emphasis will have beneficial effects on the singing by the audiences, and in training song leaders.

There is another type of worthwhile course of instruction in singing for congregations which should be called to your attention. It is what I sometimes call a "singing meeting." One brother who is a wonderful instructor in this type of work calls it a "Music Appreciation Series." In some respects, it is better for a church than an ordinary, old-time "do-re-mi" singing school. This spends little time on actual notes and learning the rudiments, since in many places more and more of the children are getting that in the public schools. But this type of program specializes in training the people to observe the principles of music written into the songs with which they are generally acquainted. It does deal with a minimum of principles as to notes, etc., but stresses the "Music Appreciation".

1. Instructs a congregation as to interpreting the songs, expressing the various sentiments and themes.
2. Deals with starting and stopping together.
3. Following the leader, regardless of what he does.
4. Proper leading by the song directors.
5. Observing the proper time, and too many other points to mention here.

To those of us who already know the rudiments, this is worth more to a church than a regular rudiments school. But people need to know the rudiments, and song leaders are very, very limited in their usefulness if they are not thoroughly acquainted with these principles. Once mastering the rudiments, or even if they do not know them, churches will find great profit in this newer type of "Singing Meeting," or "Music Appreciation Series." Either type, of course, will tremendously benefit a church, if taught by one who knows his business.

We are suffering over the brotherhood more from a scarcity of capable song leaders, I believe, than in any other department of leadership. We find, in most of the congregations, so many men who have good voices and could be splendid leaders, but they know nothing about the rudiments of music; they seem to think they cannot learn, and they are indifferent to exerting the necessary effort to learn. And many of them are pitifully unaware of how they butcher the music when they lead. The trend in some quarters to eliminate training of song leaders and employ one trained man to lead all of the singing may temporarily improve the singing in those particular spots, but it portends a poverty of song leaders and a wholesale drying up of leaders in all phases of the work. A church may find itself for the time being forced to resort to such measures. If made a permanent policy, however, it destroys development of song leaders within the congregation. That can bring evil, and only evil, in the years to come.

III. Daily Vacation Bible School.

I am ashamed to acknowledge that I grew interested in this phase of church work only in recent years. I have always been busy, but, for some queer reason, I never got busy with the DVBS until later years. Now, I confess, I lost many golden opportunities. I had no objections to it, but never seriously considered it. All of this is my way of saying, the DVBS can mean so much to the church that you should begin at once, if you have not already done so, to stress this part of the church's work.

A. Here are some advantages in this work.
   1. It will reach more outsiders, many children coming from homes of the world who will not at first otherwise attend our services. Many churches have faithful members who were led to the Gospel through this very means.
   2. The DVBS will be a good tonic for the congregation, both in providing concentrated instruction in God's Word and in causing the church to be stimulated by this extraordinary effort.
   3. It will be a great stimulant toward developing teachers and helpers. And when I speak of developing teachers, I mean both those who are experienced and inexperienced. Since so many lessons are packed into so short a time (usually two classes per day for at least a week, and maybe two weeks), the DVBS provides hard work and special preparation exceeding that of the usual Sunday classes. This is not because there should be less work for a given class on Sunday than during the DVBS, but because

between Sundays, a teacher has an entire week for immediate preparation; during the DVBS, there is little time between days and classes on each day. Both teachers and pupils do more work and receive as much instruction in a six-days DVBS (which is what we customarily have—Monday through Saturday) as in the ordinary Sunday Bible school for three months—and usually more, for we have two classes of full forty-five minutes daily in the DVBS, and many Sunday Bible schools do not have actually forty-five minutes to a given class. I do not detract from or reflect upon the teachers of the weekly, Sunday classes when I say that, but by the very nature of the case, the teachers from the DVBS have to work harder and make more intensive preparation for that endeavor than for any other period of teaching work in a church's yearly calendar. Veteran teachers make more progress; less experienced ones take longer strides in teaching efficiency; helpers and novices move closer into the fold of being teachers able to proceed on their own, and they gain greater confidence. Every DVBS in which I participate makes me see these values more clearly and provokes amazement within me that I did not begin earlier in life to push this type of work.
  4. It provides a stimulant to the church's activity at the very time—summer—when affairs usually are on the drag.
B. Let us list just a few points of procedure.
  1. The DVBS is largely a matter of organization.
  2. It, therefore, needs considerable planning and preparation far ahead of time.
  3. Do not hesitate to consult with others who have had experience with this work. Collect all of the written data on the subject that you can. Of late years, more of our own people have published information along this line that is very good. After you collect your material, making copious notes of what some have orally given you, study it hard, and the first thing you know, you will be an "expert" and somebody will say you are an "authority" on the subject!
  4. As many teachers and other workers, outside of the regular force of Lord's Day Bible school teachers, as is

possible should be used. That spreads work among the people. It also uncovers teaching talent of which you may not have been aware. If the congregation is too small to enable you to use all, most, or even some teachers who are not on the regular Lord's Day classes' force, at least you can usually obtain a number of helpers from the congregation who are not on the regular teaching force.
5. You will find that even if your teaching force for DVBS is smaller than is desirable, you can get along better than expected if you will have a liberal supply of helpers—people who will not necessarily have to do any teaching, but who will simply help to attend to the children, both during class and during the play period. They will also help you with the enrolling and records.
6. Probably no one time of the summer is always best, and to be preferred in all communities. That will vary according to many conditions: locations, local programs, denominational Vacation Bible Schools, (for you would want a time when you have access to their children), congregational preferences, other special events on the annual church calendar, etc. Ordinarily I prefer mid-July. Immediately after public schools close has been considered good, but a trend is away from that, because the students have been in a nine-month's grind. Just before school opens is not bad. But plenty of advance publicity can influence people to take vacations not in mid-July during DVBS. And that time, being in the middle of summer, is difficult to excel.
7. You will find many advantages to carrying on a campaign to enroll students in the DVBS weeks in advance of it. We use a card for this purpose that also does duty as an attendance card. Before the DVBS starts, we turn the cards of those enrolled over to the various teachers. In the first class of the DVBS, a majority of the cards of the attendants are thus already filled out. Much red tape is saved. And that constant drive, many—and I do mean, many—weeks in advance of the DVBS to obtain enrollees will stimulate attendance and general interest. It is excellent promotional propaganda!

8. Make sure that you have more literature than you think you will need. It is better to have many books left over than one book too few. The cost is not as important as the souls. The literature can be so distributed as not to use all unless needed, and some publishers allow you to return unused and undamaged material for credit, or refund.
9. Do not put your teachers under too much strain in pinching pennies as to supplies and teaching aids—unless your church budget absolutely forces you to do so. In that case, try to raise the money among the members. A plentiful supply of such materials will increase the effectiveness of the school beyond estimation.
10. Keep adequate records, but do not smother your workers with too much detail. Have the pupils' cards filled out accurately and completely. Have someone in each class as secretary, responsible for the records. Have a general secretary to whom all the class records go. Let your records tell, among other things, the church affiliation or church family background of each pupil. This will be helpful for follow-up work, both among outsiders and in the congregation.
11. Here is a suggested daily program for your DVBS, which we regularly use, with only slight variations:
    a. 9:00-9:15 A.M., Opening Assembly (15 minutes)
    b. 9:15-10:00 A.M., First Class (45 minutes)
    c. 10:00-10:20 A.M., Recreation and Refreshments (20 minutes)
    d. 10:20-11:05 A.M., Second Class (45 minutes)
    e. 11:05-11:30 A.M., Final Assembly (25 minutes)

    This totals two and one-half hours. In this schedule, the opening assembly is a brief devotional period, with the boys doing as much as possible, and with such brief announcements as are necessary to get the day's work under way. The school should start and stop promptly on time. Actually, 15 minutes will hardly be needed for this devotional, so that the students can really be in their classes by 9:10. The period of 20 minutes for recreation and refreshments should be ample, if properly organized and executed. The final assembly can be used in every moment with songs, group drills, and someone should be in charge of this who has the program fully in hand and knows how to execute it. Class reports for the day should be given. In this suggested program, you may find many ways that you prefer to change it. But we have used this several times, and we have not had a poorly attended school or day, very few (if any) dull moments, with enthusiasm on every day. We always have an adult class, which helps the school in several ways.

    I would urgently recommend that you push this DVBS work. Try to have it made a regular part of the program of the church where you preach. If I had to choose between a program of having two meetings annually and no Vacation Bible School, and a program of one meeting and the DVBS, I would choose the latter program as benefitting the church far more in the long run. Actually, a good DVBS during the summer will make a fall protracted meeting a better one, as well as contributing to the progress of the church over the whole year. By all means, try it.

CHAPTER 12
DEVELOPING THE CHURCH IN WORK PART 2

A Gospel preacher, working full time with a congregation, should major on training that church in work. He is not employed to do anyone's work. While he gives full time to the work, a part of his task is developing the members of the congregation, individually and as a group, in work. That is why three lectures are devoted to this subject. And again, we deal with the actual mechanics of carrying on specific projects. In our preceding lecture, we studied the matter of a preacher developing that church in a visitation program, training classes (public speaking classes, singing schools, special teachers courses), and daily vacation Bible schools.

I. Church Bulletins.

Church bulletins are receiving more and more attention, and deservedly so. Some men "got set" before these bulletins became so popular, and they never will become interested in such "gadgets." Some could not do much with the bulletins if they tried. But bulletins for churches are becoming the rule rather than the exception. There is no doubt in my mind that they are highly useful, but I am also convinced that they are almost necessary. I would not quite say that, but I think so much of their value that I would not stop far from stating the case in that way. My advice to you would be to study how to use them, and then use them.

    A. To have a successful church bulletin, the very first point to establish is: what is its purpose? The purpose of the church bulletin is fourfold.

        1. It is to teach Gospel truth. It should not be confined to news and "vital statistics," but should include

some direct and profitable teaching. That can be accomplished, regardless of the size and frequency. I have seen some very fine bulletins which do no direct teaching, but are devoted exclusively to news and statistics. But my conviction is that they are losing some very great potential power. Brief, direct teaching, both to world and church, will add punch and profit to the church bulletin. Such opportunities for good should not be wasted.

2. The bulletin's purpose is to inform the church and world as to the particular work of the congregation. The more a congregation knows about its work, the more work it will do. When people are kept in the dark as to what goes on, they do not have that personal interest which they would have if they were better posted. The various details are of more interest than we sometimes think, and often the smallest details can be the most interesting. But those out in the world who receive the bulletin need to know about the work of the church. They need to realize that we have standards, ideals, aims, and certain procedures. All of that increases their admiration for the church. And to know how that work is done in line with New Testament directives gives more information which is needed.

3. A purpose of the bulletin is to stimulate the church to service. Action is the aim of all teaching, of course. It is inevitable that a bulletin which has teaching and information will stimulate. The right kind of a bulletin will more than pay for itself. It will put vigor and vitality into a work. The reason some places are disappointed in their bulletins is because the bulletins have a very poor grade of workmanship. Often they are below par in appearance and/or lacking in punch as to material. They make no impression for good. But you will find that a bulletin or church paper that is a good mechanical job, and which has material that is worthy to be read, will certainly stir and stimulate more activity in the church. There are members of the church who do not know that, who know little or nothing about the mechanics of building up a congregation, or who may know much of this, but who are simply uninformed on this feature of that

work; they will argue that a bulletin is not worth the time or cost necessary to its publication. Do not be discouraged by such people. Try to have a bulletin or paper; make an effort to have a good one; and be patient to wait for results. You will see that it will create enough interest to say that it is serving its purpose to stimulate.

4. Your bulletin should seek to convert. If you have some teaching in it, it should be influential in teaching people. We have always, as a people, argued for the power of the seed as it is sown in the human heart. We have stressed the fact that it will bear fruit in time. We have made much of the point that often the Word spoken or sown may appear to accomplish nothing, but that it may spring up a long time later and in the least expected place. We have specialized in this argument in meetings where there were no baptisms. Well, why will not these points apply to the sowing, the scattering of the Word by means of the printed page? If so, why not apply this principle to the teaching in your bulletin? Just as teaching in your bulletin may influence a member of the church in a way of which you are not aware, by the same token that teaching may affect an alien sinner in such a way as to lead to his ultimate conversion. Always keep in mind that one purpose of your church bulletin or paper is to convert people to Christ.

Let us summarize these purposes of a church bulletin or paper. This can be stated in four words: teach, inform, stimulate, and convert. You can always accomplish more in any field of activity if you know what your aims are, and keep them everlastingly before you. If you will make these four aims the purpose of your church bulletin or paper, you will improve the standard of your bulletin, and you will see it being worth more for the church which pays to have it printed.

B. Next, let us notice the content. Your aims, purposes, and objectives in publishing a church bulletin or paper will be the determining factor in deciding what material shall go into your publication.

1. If one aim is to teach the Gospel, then certainly there will be articles directed toward the world.

2. If your bulletin or paper also seeks to inform and stimulate the church to service to Christ, surely articles directed to the church should be included. It will be good for both the members and non-members to read articles peculiarly applicable to each group.

For example, alien sinners need to be taught how to become Christians and the nature of the church they are entering. They also need to know the standards of life, worship, and work which Christ expects of Christians. But Christians need the "indoctrination" found in articles directed toward the world. And Christians need constant instruction in character, conduct, worship, and work. Why any preacher or church would have any sort of a bulletin without articles on such subjects is a mystery to me. The size of the bulletin will determine the amount of space to be devoted to such articles. But I see two hurtful extremes among church bulletins and papers: some have nothing but news items, "personals," and copy of such nature; others have none of that, devote all of their space to articles, and sometimes one article consuming an entire bulletin. The best way I know to keep your bulletin from being read is to let one article take up the whole issue. And the surest way I know to make it lightweight, and lose made-to-order opportunities to exert powerful influence through teaching, is to fill it up with personal items, news of the work, and statistics, and have no direct teaching. Surely between the two—the weighty and forbidding, all-teaching extreme on one hand, and that of the light extreme of all-news composition on the other—there should be a happy medium. Let your readers grow accustomed to looking for some straight, solid, but brief, teaching on Bible subjects in each issue, as well as personal and work news.

And let us not make the mistake of merely filling up space with quotations from others. It is permissible, proper, and profitable to use entire articles and brief quotes, including single sentences, from others. But there is such a thing as going to an extreme on that. The writer of a bulletin or paper who will never use a quotation from other writers indicts and proves himself guilty of conceit. He may not be aware of it, but the verdict stands. And he deprives his readers of variety, and his material of bolstering which is available and worthwhile. But the one who principally uses quotes from others betrays a woeful lack of mental energy and deprives the readers of the due influence of his own personality. Again, we want to seek to maintain a sensible balance. Doubtless any of us could collect a considerable amount of quotations and articles which would surpass anything that we could write. But your readers will still be interested in what you will write, for various personal and local reasons. So, do your own writing, with just enough supplementary material from others to give variety, strength, and expansion to your own articles and notes.

3. There is also vital news. We include in this category all items of interest about people, statistics, and the actual work of the church. The length and relative proportion of all of this will depend upon the size and nature of your bulletin, or paper. Sometimes a bulletin "goes to seed" in figures. Statistical charts can be interesting to a few who have special interest in such, but too much of that will repel the average reader. Try to hold your records to a necessary minimum. In that way, they will more likely be read, digested, and applied. News about the work of the congregation is interesting and helpful in accomplishing your aim to inform and stimulate the church to greater service.

As to personal news, my sincere judgment is that much of such news in church bulletins is waste and froth. For example, why consume valuable space in a church bulletin by making mention of the various trips and vacations of the members? Why use up space with a list of all who visited your services? Your church bulletin is not a county newspaper, trying to tell all who visit and where, all who were visited and by what people, who was gone Sunday, and why and where. Yes, people love to see their names in print. But is a church bulletin or paper to be built on a foundation of appealing to and encouraging vanity in people?

Why not use only such personal news as is really news and which will serve some worthwhile New

Testament purpose? My own practice is to mention some "personal" items, but dealing only with such sickness as is more than common (and I don't mean, the common cold), deaths, weddings, births, and a few other items of general interest which will serve a definite and good purpose—such as a shower, which is a social project and which will promote fellowship in many ways. But all of the foregoing can be held to a minimum of space and the barest details.

C. But what of the appearance of the bulletin? It simply must be neat and attractive—first grade of paper, with print that is good, clear and appropriate. It should be printed, if the church is able to bear that expense. But a mimeographed job can be done creditably, if one will take the time and trouble to do so. Many mimeographed bulletins are on a sorry grade of paper, the letters are not clear, and the general appearance is "lousy." It would be better if such a job had never been put out. When you are putting your bulletin out on a mimeograph machine, or the equivalent, and some sheets come through which are not properly inked and clear, destroy them, and do not insult your readers by sending them papers that are sorry in appearance and difficult to read. Money spent on the best grade of paper, as well as all materials and equipment, is money profitably invested. Bulletins sent out which are second-class, or worse, in appearance do more damage than good, regardless of what words of wisdom may be printed on the pages.

D. As to coverage, it is many times more effective if they are mailed, and not distributed at the church building. The coverage in mailing is one-hundred percent thorough. That more than pays for the added cost. The mailing list should include all church families, prospects, some other friends, and exchanges with many other church bulletins. This policy enables you to reach so many more with your bulletin than if you merely hand it out. Ordinarily, people do a better job of reading it if it comes to them at home through the mail. Narrow penny-pinching as to coverage will not save the church money, but will cost money—and souls—in the long run. Churches which mail their bulletins (assuming that they publish bulletins worthy of the name and worth being read) are finding that the cost of mailing is compensated many times by

the effect on attendance, contributions, and souls influenced.
E. As to frequency—congregational willingness and ability, the type of program itself, and your own available time will all have a bearing on this point. The ideal is a weekly distribution. Twice per month is the next best. Monthly is better than none at all. There is no way to lay down a universal rule on this point, because of so many different factors being involved at different places. But it is always desirable to issue it as often as possible and practical.
F. Regularity in mailing should be a MUST. There should be a regular time to mail, or distribute, and you should NEVER vary from that time. If you can have the right kind of help to publish the bulletin in your absence (the machine and mailing work), you can write the copy in advance of your out-of-town meetings and other trips. There will be some deviation from the normal pattern of the content, but this can preserve the bulletin going out on schedule in your absence. That will be worth the effort, if you can obtain dependable help to make it possible. If your help is not dependable and/or efficient, then it would be better just to omit publishing it when you are gone. But regularity will pay.

In the final analysis, the church paper or bulletin (call it what it is) can be a great tool for the progress of the congregation and the teaching of outsiders. You should study the art of publishing one, and make it a strong force in your work as a Gospel preacher. Try to get some regular and efficient help. Write the copy yourself, but try to enlist members in the congregation to do the mechanical and mailing work. That will cut down on the work you will have, for you will have plenty to do anyway, and it will give more work for others to do. I have spent so much time on this part of our work because it is something of a hobby with me, and I believe that it is impossible to overestimate the good that can be done by the church bulletin or paper. Members and non-members will read those papers and bulletins if you will make them interesting, attractive, and filled with some solid meat.

II. **Tracts.**

Keep good tracts on hand. They should be a permanent and essential part of your work. Never should a congregation be without them. Their value is not debatable among people who have kept themselves informed in the progress of different religious groups. There are some matters which we concede to be questions of judgment, with the possibility of value or uselessness being on either side of the controversy. Not so with the question of tracts. Their worth has been positively demonstrated by every conceivable cult. They have sown the country down with their tracts, and have reaped multitudes of members thereby.

You should pay close attention to the kind of tracts you have for the use of workers. They should not be too bulky or long. Of course, judgment varies at this point. But most people who have used them for any length of time will tell you that they should be comparatively brief, but not painfully so. Few people read the very long articles in our religious papers, and the average man will not read the very long tract. The tracts which I write and have printed were written for a 9-inch by 4-inch folder, 4 pages. Though the form has varied, the amount remains the same.

Write them yourself, if you can do so. The local preacher's name means more to the community than the name of some far off author. If you feel that you simply cannot write them, then carefully check and select those that you use. Avoid for general use those that are written as if the writer were in a debate. There is a place for the religious debate, in which opposition is smothered, but tracts of that nature should be reserved for special occasions. I believe that there are places and times in which religious debates are valuable, and even essential. But the usual debater's style is not the most desirable one for general preaching or for general tract distribution. Under the best of conditions, the debate is in the nature of a contest. Even though the motives of the Gospel preacher are to reach deceived, lost souls with the truth, in contrasting truth with error, still the nature of combat is in the debate. But tracts for general distribution to the world should be written in a spirit of explaining to an honest outsider what the Bible teaches, and, therefore, what we of the churches of Christ stand for, and why. Many honest people in the world are bewildered. Many of them sincerely seek information. Your tracts should be in the spirit of discussing those questions with such people—the very same spirit as that which should characterize the most of your preaching. Sometimes, you have to perform a "major operation" in opposing an evil influence, either in or out of the church. But that attitude, which is sometimes so necessary and which I certainly do not shrink from when I feel it is necessary, and the attitude of putting to flight a sectarian preacher in debate—such attitudes, I say, are not those to be found in your general preaching and in your tracts which are widely distributed among the public on most subjects. Hence, if you use tracts in developing the congregation in work, as you certainly should, be just as careful about the spirit of those tracts as the doctrine.

Have a good tract rack, or cabinet, displayed in a prominent place, where the members can easily get to the tracts. The more convenient you make it for the members to reach for those tracts, the more likely the tracts are to be used. Keep the tracts publicized before the church. Make frequent announcements, from the pulpit, in class, in your bulletin. You and other "personal workers" will continually use them. Since about 1936, I have kept a series of these tracts, written by myself, before the congregations, on a number of subjects. They deal with most of the questions which the world loves to throw at members of the body of Christ. They constitute what I love to think of as a strong course in "indoctrination." I have noticed that every time we have a service, or a class, members go to the tract cabinet and obtain various subjects. That has convinced me that the members will use these effective tools if they are properly and constantly reminded and urged. The best of the members forget, and need to have it often called to their attention. One effective way to do this is to keep before them exactly what subjects are there. So many of them will not take the trouble to search for what they want, to see if it is there—though some members will keep the whole set on hand. But if they are told that certain subjects are there, they then will go for that special item while it is fresh on their minds.

While we are being careful that the tracts teach sound doctrine, and in the right spirit, do not overlook the importance of having them printed on a good grade of paper. Dirty, faded, poorly-printed copy does more damage than good. It does not save money to get cheap tracts. It costs money. First-class paper and printing give them a better approach to the hearts of prospective readers and increase the prospect's respect for the church's estimate of what it asks the prospect to read.

In the final analysis, the tracts will do four things in developing the church in work:
  A. Teach and sometimes convert aliens.
  B. Indoctrinate the church.
  C. Stimulate the members to take more interest in contacting people.
  D. Give the members a useful tool with which to do the work of teaching people the truth. So often, there are members who are very deficient in knowing how to explain the truth of the Bible to people. Just as a sermon helps them to understand it and better explain it, so do the tracts. And the most efficient members can find the tracts a great help. In addition to any talking done by a member to a prospect, if a tract or some tracts can be left, the prospect will often read and study them in the privacy of the home.

So, keep a liberal supply of tracts. We have always urged the power of the seed as it is sown, that it may spring up in the form of a plant at the least expected place and time. That is the history of Gospel tracts. You will find that they will have a far reaching influence on the church directly and on those aliens who live in the community.

CHAPTER 13

DEVELOPING THE CHURCH IN WORK PART 3

In my work as a Gospel preacher, employed to devote a major portion of my time with a particular congregation, for years I have featured a slogan which runs like this: develop a church that is (1) sound in doctrine, (2) clean in life, (3) friendly in spirit, and (4) aggressive in work. Because this course of lectures, to the student-preachers of this college, deals principally with the fourth feature of that platform does not mean that we are to ignore the other three. It just happens that we are here dealing with the everyday "mechanics" of doing the work of a preacher with a congregation. For that reason, three of these lectures are devoted to the theme of "Developing The Church In Work." Further, while all of the other speeches in this course of studies deal with the work, as such, in these three, we are stressing certain specific points in which you should try with all of your might to develop that church as a worker. In the two preceding lectures, we have given attention to the following: developing a visitation program, training classes (public speaking classes, special teachers' courses, singing schools), daily vacation Bible schools, church bulletins or papers, and tracts. Now we study these: using all of your talents among the members, young people's meetings on Sunday nights, a year-round Wednesday night program, and your attitude toward various institutions and movements (religious journals, Christian colleges and secondary schools, orphanages, homes for aged, and all "special appealers").

I. Using All of the Talent in Work and Public Worship.

A. Make a special effort to see that all proper men, young men, and boys in the church are used in public work and worship. Others may—and should—look after these details. It is not best for the preacher to be forced to attempt to handle all details. Sometimes he is forced to do so because of the scarcity of men, or the failure of the proper ones to assume their rightful responsibilities. But, under normal conditions, there are others in the congregation who will do either all, most, or much of the selecting of the various ones to attend to particular tasks. And even though other brethren will attend to the actual operation of this part of the work, you should still make that a personal and special study, and give your personal attention to helping those in charge to see that this is done, and that it is done right.
B. Too often it is a case of "the same old six and seven." Even in some larger congregations, the brethren get into a rut and call on about the same crowd all of the time to pass the emblems, usher (if such a thing is ever done), lead singing, lead prayers, read Scriptures, etc. Often the brethren excuse themselves for this rut by crying that "we can't get others to do this work." Certainly I would agree that there are men who simply will not budge, who will not do one thing along this line, and they will be like that the next time you inquire or hear of them. They whimper that they would do it if no one else would, but "there are others so much better qualified." By a refusal to take part and train themselves in this work, they deprive themselves of that growth that could be theirs and rob the church of a more efficient quality of performers if and when they are ever forced to take a public part. In nearly all cases, this is indifference and sleepishness of the deadest sort. Sometimes these "Let-George-do-it" fellows can be thawed out and something made out of them. Sometimes, the case is hopeless.
C. But of one thing I am quite certain: this condition of using the same comparatively small crowd can nearly always be improved if you will stay after the problem. If you will give a special study to this, and concentrate your efforts on it, you will greatly stimulate the development of leaders in the church. That, in turn, will give freshness, new feelings, and life to the whole church. Search the list of men, young men, and boys in the church roll as you

would hunt for that proverbial "needle in the haystack," and give everyone a chance to be doing something. One will respond to the call of one job, and another to that of a different type. But, above all, see that all of the members, as nearly as possible, have something specific to do. Many men and boys have been led along, step-by-step, from either passing songbooks to people, ushering, or passing emblems, to occupying the pulpit in the absence of the regular preacher. If you find yourself located with a large old church, having more talent than can be used, and indifferent to any training program, still I would urge you to have faith that development can come if the effort is wisely and persistently made. And it matters not how much talent is in that church, there is still a need to carry on such an effort. Some old and large churches are fossilizing and do not know it. They are like the church to whom Christ said, "...thou...knowest not that thou art wretched, and miserable, and poor, and blind, and naked." (Rev. 3:17)

D. Perhaps I should explain the use of the word proper in the first sentence of this topic, under section A. By "all proper men, young men, and boys in the church," I am acknowledging that some cannot be used because of their character and influence. People become nauseated upon seeing men or young men passing the emblems of the Lord's Supper who are known to be drinkers, cursers, gamblers, dancers, or adulterers. We have to draw a line. It is true that some of the congregations are drifting into worldliness and have no standards whatever along this line. You will note this history of the case: those churches which first let the bars down, and will use only the dancers in a public capacity, will—and do—eventually reach the place where they will thus use adulterers, gamblers, and profane men of the most notorious type. They drift step-by-step. But the men need to be plainly told that the church cannot use such characters in any public capacity, just as some of their mothers, wives, and sisters need to be forbidden to teach classes as long as they practice or condone the same worldly and evil conduct. These people who teach classes need not only to refrain personally from such evils, but also to teach against and use their total influence against such practices. When pulpits and other Christian homes stand squarely against these—and other—worldly actions, they and their children do not deserve to be sabotaged in classes by teachers who do not sound a clear tone in their call to opposition against these evils. The stand of no teacher should be in the least doubt in the minds of all students in every class. Any other course justifies the conversion of that teacher, or his or her replacement! Such talent so destroys its influence for good that you dare not use it—unless you have abandoned the distinctive character of the church as taught in the New Testament and practiced by us through the years. (2 Cor. 6:14-18; Rom. 12:2; Gal. 5:19-21; Eph. 5:3-5; Matt. 7:20) Many elderships seem to have no standards along this line, but will use any sort of a known worldly character in a public capacity. Some elders do have convictions right here, but are too weak to express vigorous objection when one in charge of that part of the work enforces no standards. Certainly, as preachers, you cannot force the elders to do as you know the New Testament teaches. But you can do your best to try to teach them and the church the principles of the foregoing Scriptures, and you can show how that to use such people in public capacity or positions of responsibility in the church helps to destroy those principles. It is a mistake to say: "If we use such people, it will help to bring them out of worldly practices." Instead, it puts the church's endorsement on such and says: "You can dance, drink, gamble, live in adultery, dress immodestly or indecently, (1 Tim. 2:9) etc., and take a public and teaching part in the church's work." It says that to others in the audiences and classes. A wonderful influence that is for a New Testament church! But get ready for real opposition, young men, from many members—and even from those in high places—when you take a position like that. So, first make up your mind as to where you stand."

Where the character and influence of the men and boys are such that you are at liberty to use them, the more you use all of that talent, the more you cause them to feel a part of the work, the more you will encourage others to take part, the more variety you will have, the less of a rut you will find the church in, the more you will find those taking part will go on and develop in other and greater ways, and the more spirituality you will generate in all of the worship and work of the church. Make this one of your points of special stress.

II. Young People's Meeting on Sunday Night.

A. In some places, you will not have this problem. Sometimes, the hours for the night worship services make impractical a Sunday night young people's meeting. In other places, there may be opposition to such a meeting. In that case, "take it easy." Elsewhere, there may be no active opposition, but no particular interest. Considerable time may be required to create sufficient interest in such a program. Or, you may be at a place where special circumstances—either history or immediate conditions—may render such a meeting inadvisable for the time being. Let circumstances govern your procedure. Even so, though you are where there is no such program, and cannot be for a long time, some day you will face the problem and have to assume personal responsibility for its success. For that reason, you should study the matter and develop some definite ideas along this line.

B. Here are some guiding principles to consider in the Sunday night young people's meeting.

1. Make it solid, and not "frothy." It should not be just an excuse for a social gathering and fun of that type. Social "get-togethers" for the young people, in my judgment, serve a useful purpose and should be promoted. We ask our young people to stay away from the modern dance and related evil places and often do nothing to provide a legitimate association with other young people. But the Sunday night young people's meeting is not for that purpose. Neither is it to be simply an excuse or means of keeping the young people away from denominational young people's meetings. It should be used to give sound and practical instruction in Christianity. It has been my experience, without exception where I have tried it, that the young people WILL respond to and take an interest in that type of a program. He who says that they will not, because they want something lighter, simply does not know how to present something solid in a way which the young people will accept. It can be done, and it is being done in many, many places.

2. The meeting should always be thoroughly planned.

Sometimes, they just drift along, with little planning, and people then wonder why they die. If a church is to have a meeting of this type, it is not one merely to be tolerated and not to be seriously treated.
3. It should be regular, and not spasmodic. Sometimes, they are canceled for the most trivial causes—such as, if the teacher wants to be away, or actually must be. But a substitute should always be prepared, so that the meeting will continue without so much as a single interruption. If these meetings are sometimes called off, you will have confusion, and that will be another contributing cause to death.
4. Consider that the Sunday night young people's meeting, or class, affords you an opportunity to give those young people something in the way of indoctrination and training, and to wield an influence over them that will be felt for all time. It may be that you will find it possible, and profitable, to have several classes on Sunday night, instead of merely one for the young people. More and more congregations are turning to this plan. In the first place, we need all of the Bible classes possible and practical, without being unreasonable in our demands along that line. Before the Sunday night service is usually a good time for such an additional program. If you have a young people's class, you will often find some of the parents and younger children coming, or visiting around in the community after bringing their young people to the meeting, so no hardship would be worked on them to ask them to come to classes. If, then, you are able to have a program of several classes on Sunday night before your assembly worship, or if you can only have the one young people's class, or meeting, treat that program as an opportunity and not as drudgery.

III. A Practical, Year-round Wednesday Night Program.
A. What to do on Wednesday night, seems to be a difficult problem with many churches. You can preach to people until you are blue in the face that they should attend the Wednesday night service, but your preaching will have more effect if you have a constructive program to assist in drawing them there, and keeping them after they are drawn. I believe that it is their duty to attend. The com-

mand of Heb. 10:25 does not confine itself to the Lord's Supper service. He who says that it means only the Lord's Supper, or any Lord's Day service, just reads into the text what is not stated. The text says "assembling," and it does not confine the obligation to any one assembly. Certainly, then, you are at liberty to urge that text as a Divine command not to forsake ANY assembly. Further, the urge to "grow in grace and knowledge" (2 Pet. 3:18), the "hunger and thirst after righteousness" (Matt. 5:6), the matter of being established "in every good work and word" (2 Thess. 2:17), the principle of being an example before others (Phil. 2:15), the principle of all members of the body working together (1 Cor. 12:12-27), with other principles and dozens of other New Testament Scriptures, all combine to lay upon all members, able to attend, the obligation to attend all services and classes of the church. You can preach these points, have a poorly arranged program on Wednesday night, and have some to attend. But you can preach these points, present an interesting program on Wednesday night, and have many more to attend. Sometimes, we take the people to task for not attending, when those responsible for the program are the ones to be taken to task for such slovenly planned work.

B. Let me suggest a year-round plan. With very few years as exceptions, I have used this arrangement since 1932. In the very few years when the plan in its entirety was not used, we had a modified version of it. And in those 28 years, it has been uniformly received with favor, with the attendance in each place steadily climbing. Of course, sometimes what will fit in one place will not fit at another—at least, in the first of your work. Because of the varying size of congregations, and the differing amounts of talent available in each place, as well as other factors unnecessary to mention now, you may be forced to trim or alter any plan to fit your place. But usually we can develop a church into the ability to use a plan, so here it is.

1. In fall, winter, and spring—Bible classes. The number, the starting and stopping times, etc., must depend upon necessary circumstances. Avoid having too many classes, but try just enough to maintain necessary age classifications. Do your best to have a different set of teachers from the ones you use on

Sundays. Sometimes this is impossible. Sometimes there must be some duplication. In that case, it is usually desirable for the teachers to have different classes on Sunday morning and Wednesday night, except in some specialized groups where only one teacher is qualified to teach in that field. Avoid having too much overlapping between the courses of study on Sundays and Wednesdays. If someone says that "to have Bible classes on Sunday mornings, Sunday nights, and Wednesday nights is having too many classes," let him or her take pencil and paper and figure the hours spent by young people during the week in secular classes, and the maximum they could spend in Bible classes if they attended every one, and then watch the face get red—unless he or she has the stubborn kind of a face that doesn't ever grow red, even though proved wrong!

2. In summer—a general program. Abolish classes when school is out, and for the summer have the whole group to meet in one assembly for the entire period each night. Have songs with different leaders. Have a few more prayers than customary. Assign a few Scripture readings. Have from one to three short talks—and I mean short talks. If one is able, have someone appointed to drill the audience in a new song. That will add freshness and stimulation to the singing. In this program, use as many men, young men, and boys in the church as will take part. You can vary this summer program to fit the amount of talent you have available.

C. This arrangement has many values.
1. It gives variety, and in the best proportion. The people, especially the children and young people, appreciate the classes, but by the time the summer general program comes, they are ready for it. They move into the summer program with interest, looking forward to something different. They enjoy the summer program, and appreciate the men and boys who take part. But when the fall comes, they are then ready for the class program, and they dive into it with zest.
2. The plan provides worship in the assembly, the essentiality of which we all recognize.
3. This plan provides much teaching of God's Word.

At best, the amount of class teaching we receive is distressingly small. And the teaching of this plan is spread over the whole year, but arranged in different sections—classes and talks.

4. The plan also affords a great amount of developing in public work and worship. It carries on the work of training men, young men, and boys. If you have a night public speaking class, you will see more immediate fruits of that part of your program in this Wednesday night program. This plan also supplies more opportunities to develop teachers, as they teach in classes. It schools a church in proper singing. In short, this year-round Wednesday night program presents an ideal combination of worship, instruction, training, and general internal development of a congregation.

IV. Attitude Toward Institutions and Movements Originating Outside the Congregation Where you Preach.

In introducing this part of this lecture, let us make some matters crystal clear. I am not about to advocate that we tie any institution to or fasten it on the church. To "institutionalize the church" is one of the last things we propose to do. But, because of certain controversies in progress, many sincere brethren have been foolishly driven to be hostile to some enterprises because of a mistaken notion of institutions. The Merriam-Webster Dictionary defines an institution as "an established society or corporation, esp. one of a public character." Any company publishing a Gospel journal is an institution. So is a Christian college. So is a corporation publishing a religious book. It is not my aim to fasten any of these institutions upon the church as such. Because I believe that such institutions may be supported by individual Christians under proper conditions and safeguards does not mean that "institutionalizing the church" is favored; and because some are carrying on such a war on this issue does not justify us in being stampeded into opposing any and all "institutions" under any conditions.

Further, I am not here going into as much detail in discussing these controversies as some might wish. In some cases, conditions among us of the past few years justify me, I sincerely believe, in going into more detail than in some other instances. I shall clearly state my position on these "institutions"—as should any other Gospel preacher, teacher, elder, or public servant. Because in some instances I do not spend as much time exploring points of the controversies as in other cases, does not mean that I fear to give my reasons for such. Nor does it mean that I believe you should accept the sentiments here expressed simply because I advocate them. There are debates on these issues published in book form, where you may find them debated in detail. I fully stand with and endorse the position taken by Brother Guy N. Woods in the Woods-Porter Debate and the Woods-Cogdill Debate, published by the Gospel Advocate Co., on orphan homes and congregational cooperation in such matters as Herald of Truth. That should make my position clear enough. And a little further along in this lecture you will see obvious and personal reasons why I felt impelled to enter into the orphan home question in a more detailed way. But this course of lectures was planned to deal with doing the work and not arguing the many points of controversy that may be related; I mention these controversial matters, such as colleges, orphan homes, and papers, not so much to argue their justification as to help you in governing your procedure in assisting them; and I clearly state my attitude toward them so that no one can say that "he is afraid to tell where he stands." I recognize that to mention these matters in this speech, if this goes into a book, will close some doors to the book and restrict its sales. But I am more interested in assisting student preachers, and others who hear and read, than I am in selling the book. And you may quote me on that and sign my name.

  A. First, let us consider religious journals published by our brethren.
     1. I believe that they have a right to exist, individually and not church owned, if they are commercial enterprises engaging in secular business.
     2. Certainly, they do much good, the extent of which cannot be estimated. The printed page goes to Christian and non-Christian, and both are thereby influenced.
     3. The best ones among us occasionally do some harm, for they are no more perfect than are the men who write their articles and news items. The same could be said truthfully of all of us who preach. A very, very few of these papers do more harm than good and, I sincerely believe, very little good. These are such as

specialize in attacking almost every work and person in the brotherhood—except those of their own favorite group. They are experts in rushing into print with personal attacks on brethren before obtaining all of the evidence. For example, a newspaper will carry a story about a brother "observing Easter." The newspaper clipping finds its way to a writer for this paper. Without consulting the brother and learning if the newspaper account was correct, he writes an article lambasting his brother for "observing Easter." Later evidence proves the brother did no such thing, neither the church with which he labored, and the newspaper report was false. But the damage was done, and many readers of that "religious" paper believed the false report. There have been cases where efforts were made to persuade an editor to correct the false report, and the editor declined, or the correction was worse in its charges and implications than the original slander. This happens in one of the papers so often that it is habitual, "standard equipment." But because one or two papers make this a regular practice in representing—rather, misrepresenting—those with whom they differ, and because any paper can occasionally make mistakes, this does not warrant us in going sour on all papers published by our brethren. I know of no preacher or congregation that is entirely free of mistakes. Do you? And a few are vicious. But should we, therefore, abolish all preachers and congregations? Then let us be more sensible about our papers. There are plenty of good ones without your having to take an evil one.

4. They should be spread far and wide. Individuals and congregations may circulate Gospel papers. The paper is not an institution, though it is published by one. The church may buy papers from such an institution and circulate them, to teach the truth, just as the church may purchase from a publishing house communion trays for the use of the church. When you find a Gospel paper that is dealing with the Gospel, and not using its every issue to attack everything in the brotherhood and to stay in a wrangle with brethren, you will be doing the cause of Christ a service by giving said paper a good circulation.

5. You should not think of and use these papers as "advertising mediums."
6. You are not dependent upon the papers for work, so do not cultivate the wrong attitude here. You can have sufficient jobs and all the meetings you need if your name never appears in print in a single Gospel paper. I believe that with all of my heart.
7. But you should send to the papers reports of your work, for the sake of the interest of the report to the brotherhood. Don't you enjoy reading the reports of others? Then, others will appreciate reading your reports. The news items stimulate all of us, instruct, inspire, encourage, and inform us as to what goes on. All of us should use the news departments of the Gospel papers more than we do.
8. You should seriously and fairly consider their teaching, but remain personally independent. Remember that the New Testament is your Book of authority. Papers, as well as men, may help you. But they may also hinder you, even if not intending to do so, so avoid the attitude which so many obviously have of believing that it is so if you see it in your favorite Gospel paper.
9. Above all things, take several papers—as many as you can afford. This is more important than you might think, and you will not be wasting your money. This policy will increase your information of brotherhood affairs and trends. It will increase your storehouse of Gospel teaching by brethren. But—and I really believe this to be the most important reason for this recommendation—it will help you to remain unbiased and balanced. The preacher who reads only one commentary will usually be biased in that direction. The member who reads only one Gospel paper will nearly always be prejudiced in favor of the positions taken by that paper. Churches of Christ are damaged seriously by those who endorse about every position taken by "their" paper. Take papers which you know disagree on certain points; consider their positions and reasons, as they urge the New Testament in support thereof; but try to remain true to the New Testament, and keep your balance. Don't go off half-cocked, swallow what some writer says

about a brother, and start saying—and writing—some things of which you would later be ashamed. And don't "tear your shirt" in getting excited about some of these paper wars. We have had some rough ones, between some of our "big names," with people lining up, only later to learn that the "big names" repented of the unchristian words they applied to each other—and some did not repent. Use the papers properly, but keep your balance and get into a fight only when there is every justification for it and no justification to stay out of it. Use your own thinking, then do what you believe is right, and worry not at all about final results.

10. Occasionally file special articles or news stories. The papers want such stories. The brotherhood is profited by them.

B. Next, consider Christian colleges.
1. They have the same right to exist as do the papers, individually owned, operated, and supported.
2. It is eminently safe to keep them out of church budgets and treasuries, but to urge individuals to support them. Actually, they will receive more money from any given congregation if the contributions come from individuals as such instead of from the congregational treasury. It is my personal conviction that congregations as such should not contribute to them, but that individuals should do so. If it is not "politically expedient" to make that remark, it is still my conviction.
3. The Christian colleges have many false charges made against them.
   a. Some charge that they are created "to do the work of the church." That is no truer than it is of the Gospel papers. It is true that the papers teach truth, and so do congregations. It is true that Christian colleges teach truth. But in each case, individuals are doing that. If, because the college teaches truth, it is doing the work of the church and should be abolished, the same argument would abolish the paper. But the inconsistency right here is in the fact that the severest critics of the colleges come from some few who operate and/or write in the papers. Don't editors and

devotees of religious papers claim that Christian readers receive teaching and training in the truth, along with the secular, commercial selling of merchandise by the papers? Christian colleges teach and train in the truth as well as giving secular education to students. Religious papers teach, influence, and train preachers in the principles which they advocate. So do Christian colleges. And yet a few—a very few, thank the good Lord—papers operated by members of the church, while seeking to train and influence Gospel preachers, are the loudest critics of our colleges, claiming that they are seeking to control the preachers!!!! I devoutly trust that you never allow yourself to become so soured and poisoned in your thinking as to swallow that baseless charge about our colleges. A paper which keeps harping on that theme, and continually charges the Christian colleges with that aim, naturally lays itself liable to suspicion as to its own intent. People often consider it good strategy to divert attention from themselves by habitually harping on others. The truth of the matter is that the Christian college is created to give a secular education under Christian influence. That is the function and aim of such a school. And it is also the objective of the Christian school teaching the grades.
- b. Some charge that they exist just to train preachers. That is false. But, while they exist primarily for the purpose already named, I know of nothing wrong with young men studying the Bible and the how of becoming preachers while they are in college classes.
- c. Some often charge the schools with things of which they are not guilty, carelessly repeating rumors which have no basis in fact. The accusers often give evidence of wanting to believe the accusation. When their every utterance regarding the schools is one of condemnation, accusation, and charge, there are personal reasons for a bitterness of soul that is manifest and which colors all of their thinking on the subject.
4. Our colleges do untold good. Thousands of us have

been directly benefitted. Having graduated from David Lipscomb College (when it was a Junior college) in 1922 and from Abilene Christian College in 1924, I can testify from very personal experience of the direct benefits. I have also received many indirect benefits from those two colleges, as well as from our other Christian schools. Those who have attended no Christian school have been indirectly benefitted—and that goes for the most severe and constant critics.

5. But, being human, the schools sometimes do harm. Sometimes I have found myself objecting to certain policies and positions of some of the schools. I have not been entirely reluctant to express myself. It has not been my attitude, however, to scratch them off my list forever and permanently wage war against them as enemies of the church. It is my sincere and unreserved conviction that the wars of some years back have helped them, and that they are in their best position than at any time in their history. If the paper that carries on a constant bombardment of most of the colleges had been treated by the brotherhood because of any one of its mistakes as it has treated the schools, the paper would have folded up within a month. The same goes for some of the individual critics.

6. In spite of harm being done by the schools, as by papers and individuals, Christian education, including colleges, should be promoted. In view of their work and the position in which present day young people find themselves, I even believe that it is a duty to support and promote our Christian colleges. The very nature of the Christian college proves its value—to give a secular education under Christian teachers in every department, and in an environment of over 95 per cent of the students being Christians. Mark the efforts of Catholicism in this country to train their young people in their own schools—and then pray God to speed the day when we will learn as much as they have learned about this point. Had I the time, I would prefer to devote a whole lecture to the subject of our duty to support our Christian colleges.

7. But avoid blind loyalty to the institution, regardless.

This is a definite menace among us. We have seen instances of ex-students defending the policies of their schools, when such policies were in clear violation of truth. When the school got straight on the issue, the partisan defenders still resented the objections to the college position, and they will always dislike those who opposed its position. There are chronic critics who see no good in some schools and who will never be fair to them—but there are times when the staunchest lovers of the schools take issue with certain acts. So, be careful before you consign to outer darkness every critic of the college, or before you say, "My college, right or wrong." You may still love the college, though it may be wrong on a point, and try to get it right, but blind partisanship and endorsement is an evil to be shunned as the leprosy.

8. One more attitude toward the college question is this: be certain that your interest is not confined to one. There is no way, I suppose, to prevent those of us who attended various schools from being partial to those colleges. Because of associations and benefits, that probably is natural. So, I am not criticizing that. But my plea is not to confine our interest in and efforts in behalf of any one school. To the extent that they are worthy of support, support and assist any of them. And try to broaden your interests along this line, as a means of being fair, of enlarging your own heart, of enlarging the hearts of Christians whom you influence, and of being of wider service to the church.

C. Now, consider the orphanages and homes for the aged.
1. I believe that they have a right to exist. In the first edition of this book, written in 1954 and published in 1955, I took the position which I had held for years: that an orphanage and home for the aged should be under the oversight of the elders of a given congregation, that the elders should be the actual trustees, and that such homes should not be under the directorship of boards composed of brethren from various congregations. Since then I have completed a change of conviction. In order to give a full statement of the matter, I wish here to insert into the record of this book an article which I wrote for publi-

cation, and which appeared in the Gospel Advocate, of Nashville, TN, in October, 1957. The article in full follows:

"For many years it was my conviction that an orphan home, or home for the aged, to be supported by congregations of Christ and individual Christians, should be under the oversight of the eldership of a church. I even went so far as to believe that an orphanage governed by a board of brethren who were members of various congregations was comparable in principle to a missionary society. Occasionally my views were expressed in sermons and articles. In my book, The Preacher And His Work, written in 1954, published in 1955, on page 140, I stated, 'It is eminently safe that they be under the oversight of congregational elders...this plan allows contributing congregations to do so within the scriptural boundaries of Acts 11:27-30.'

"Since the church with which I have labored since September, 1952, (Homewood, Birmingham, AL) placed Childhaven (Cullman, AL) and Southern Christian Home (Morrilton, AR) in our 1957 budget, some friends over the country have wondered about my attitude, since both of these homes are governed by boards of brethren from various congregations instead of by local elderships. Articles have appeared in the Gospel Guardian and several Birmingham bulletins, featuring my former position, one writer even saying in the Guardian that '...Jack Meyer...would not join you in defending Childhaven. He says that organization is just like a missionary society.' (June 6, 1957, issue, page 1). In behalf of a clear understanding, the following is here recorded:

a. "During the past two years I have engaged in an intensive re-study of the issues involved in this question, and have been won to the changed conviction that a home such as Childhaven does not substitute for, nor compete with, the church, but does its best to restore, to stand in the place of the original home which the orphan lost. I have finally seen the point, therefore, that it is not comparable to a missionary society, for the missionary society certainly does supplant or compete with the church in preaching. John D. Cox, of Florence, AL, (Gospel Advocate, page 498, Aug. 8, 1957) exactly expresses the truth on this point which I have accepted: 'It is the responsibility of the church to provide, supply or furnish the means whereby the needy may be cared for. After the means for the care of the needy have been provided by the church, the care must still be given. This care may be provided for in the original home of the needy if it still exists, or in another private home which has taken the needy ones in, or in a substitute home which has been set up by individuals for the purpose of caring for the needy.' I believe that the obligation to provide the means of caring for the needy is ordered in the New Testament (Gal. 6:10; James 1:27; 1 Tim. 5:16), but that the method of care is not stipulated, and is thus in the realm of expediency. Therefore, I no longer hold to the view that orphanages must be under local elderships, and hereby publicly repudiate my past teaching on that point, including the quotation mentioned in my book.

b. "Our church bulletin, Homewood Visitor, goes to practically all elders, preachers, leaders, and many other church friends of Greater Birmingham."— Note; since that was published in the Gospel Advocate of October, 1957, we have eliminated from our mailing lists the anti-orphan home, anti-Herald of Truth people in Greater Birmingham, because of their constant criticism of sending it to them and because of the way they would pick paragraphs out of the bulletin and publish perversions in such a way as to make it appear that we taught and believed certain things we do not.—"During l957, I have written several articles in said bulletin, defending the right of churches to support orphanages such as Childhaven and Southern Christian Home. For example, our bulletin of April 11 referred to the decision of our elders to send $25.00 monthly to each of these homes, and made it entirely clear that I was in complete accord with that program. The writer, whose quotation in the Gospel Guardian in June represented me to the contrary, (to which I referred in paragraph 2 of this article) regularly receives our bulletin! One anti-orphan home bulletin in Birmingham conceded my change, but claimed that I had denied that I had changed—which I have not done in writing anywhere or orally to anyone at any time, since definitely completing that change last year. This I freely confess: I have been unnecessarily slow (but for no deliberate reason) in announcing through the brotherhood-wide papers my change to support such homes as Childhaven, but our bulletin has fully informed the congregations of Greater Birmingham.

c. "To find it necessary to publish a change of preaching is not the most comfortable act in the world. But it is to be preferred to stubbornly holding to error or a failure to publicly proclaim one's position. The preacher who has never changed his mind on any point is as dangerous as the one constantly vacillating—or more so.

d. "Brethren should not become discouraged by the controversy in progress over these, and other, issues. In spite of some damage, good will be the ultimate and larger end. A closer study of Bible teaching is sometimes added in the crucible of controversy. The published Woods-Porter Debate on the orphan home issue was of great value to me in the changing of convictions here announced. So were the many articles pro and con appearing in the religious papers. There is no question in my mind that the movement in opposition to orphan homes, homes for the aged, and congregational enterprises such as Herald of Truth, is based on the same foundation principles as the anti-Bible class movement, and will come to the same end. While we deplore the damage that the controversy will surely bring, out of it all we pray for a oneness in Scripture convictions among our brethren, a growing good will, a united effort and increasing emphasis upon evangelism and benevolence 'according to the pattern,' unfettered by the making of humanly-devised laws where God has made none."

And I am not one of those believing that congregations could maintain an orphanage or home for the aged only for "an emergency." When that orphan or aged person needs support, it is an emergency so far as the needy one is concerned. And to insist that such a program could be limited to a mass emergency is to make a law and read into the Scriptures a human extreme. Instead of the word "emergency," the opposers should substitute the word "need." The New Testament principle of relieving distress has always been on a basis of "distribution was made unto every man according as he had need." (Acts 4:35) As long as the need of orphans and aged people exists, I believe that churches and individuals have a right to take care of them, or that churches and individuals have the right to maintain them in homes.

Further, when you find people opposing the right of congregations to send money to support orphans in homes operated by boards of brethren who live in various places, and they make the argument that such homes are comparable to missionary societies, you will find most of these people grossly inconsistent at this point: when pressed into a corner, they will not say that it is wrong for individuals to contribute to them, that individuals may do so, but that congregations should not. Not all of the orphan home opposers will take this position, but most of them will. Well, if these "institutional" homes are comparable to missionary societies, it is tragically inconsistent to say that a church may not scripturally support them, but individuals may. Churches of Christ uniformly oppose Christians OR congregations supporting a missionary society. We do not fellowship them, nor do we fellowship those who support them. Would it be wrong for the Homewood Church of Christ to send money to the United Christian Missionary Society? We all answer: yes. Would it be wrong for an individual member of Homewood congregation to send money to that same UCMS? Again we all answer: yes. Now most of the "heavy fighters" of the orphan homes say:

Childhaven orphanage is the same as a missionary society, but in the field of benevolence; it is wrong for Homewood church to contribute to this Childhaven missionary, benevolent society; it is permissible for an individual member of Homewood church to contribute to this Childhaven missionary, benevolent society!!! Such inconsistency. Back in the days when I erroneously held to the view that only an orphanage under an eldership could be scripturally supported by churches, I never held the view that individuals could support the home under the other type board, but contended that if it was wrong for a church to contribute to it, it was likewise wrong for an individual. But not so with the "heavy guns" bombarding the orphanages. Few of them will deny the right to individuals to support them, but deny that right to churches. By what law would it be right for a Christian to contribute to a missionary society? Their inconsistency at this one major point shows how their whole position falls, and it casts some suspicion upon just how strong they are in their own avowed belief.

2. You will do well to support them. That is not the only way that orphans and aged people can be supported, but it is one way, and every Scripture arguing for helping the weak will teach our duty, to the limit of ability, to assist in this work. A congregation will be better for investing some of its money in the support of our homes for the aged and for children. And more personal interest, in addition to budgeted contributions, will also prove beneficial.

3. Yet, guard churches against "passing the buck." It is true, as the "institutional opposers" charge, that too many churches are doing in these "institutions" what they could be doing in their communities, while at the same time contributing to the support of orphanages and homes for the aged. Those of us who endorse and support such homes certainly do recognize many abuses. There are aged people shunted to such homes, who should be supported at home by their families. And there are aged people and children who could be kept in their own communities,

with the advantages of association with a strong church and their own acquaintances, but who are pushed off to the home, "at so much per." Communities lose the benefit of seeing and feeling the work of such churches and families before the eyes of the aliens. And sometimes the homes lay themselves liable to charges. All of this we can concede, and try to prevent the churches from evading their responsibilities, and at the same time see the good and support the justifiable in this part of our program. Too many chronic critics seize upon abuses to prove the error of the whole system. That plan would forever remove some critics from warting the brotherhood! And the abuse of a privilege does not prove that the privilege does not exist with justification.

D. Finally, what should be your attitude toward all "special appealers"?
   1. I mean, men wanting to come and lay before the congregation an appeal for a given project.
   2. Avoid either extreme:
      a. Being indifferent and cold to all such brethren, or
      b. Taking in all such without exercising independent judgment. I have seen preachers who were as cold as a refrigerator to anyone coming with a special appeal. They are too heartless to be accused of having the spirit of Christ. Back of that attitude is usually a selfish fear that an outsider will take out some money that will damage the work. He should know that the brethren give better support to their own resident work when they loosen up and contribute liberally to many outside appeals. Then, on the other hand, I have seen preachers go to the extreme and, with the elders, throw open the doors to any and all who came along. That policy will not only make the church bite at some dishonest and impractical schemes, but will sour the church to where they will someday swing to the other extreme.
   3. The matter of such appealers being given time before the church assembly should be cleared through the elders—and not the preacher. The preacher may suggest and urge, but the elders make the decision. That is why they are bishops-overseers.

4. Let me especially warn you on this point: some very special thought should be given to the agent who wants you to write an endorsement of a book, or to the man—perhaps even a brother—who wants you to go around with him to various brethren and sisters to help him to sell his book, or to solicit money for some other appeal. The less you can do of that, the better. It is one thing to publicly endorse and encourage any worthy work, but quite another thing to accompany a solicitor and put brethren on the spot before the solicitor by your being present as an associate solicitor. Young men, you better know what you are doing when you do that. And, when you endorse that book, be certain you are right.

The foregoing are simply some principles basic to all of such problems. These questions will sooner or later confront you, and sometimes they will plague you. So, you may as well begin to formulate procedure. I have classified these subjects under the general heading tonight of "Developing The Church In Work," knowing that they are not directly the work of the congregation, but because in your work with a church, you will be faced with what to do with these problems. And as you guide a church in its proper attitude toward these matters, you will be, after all, "developing a church in work."

CHAPTER 14
TRENDS AND CRITICAL BACKGROUNDS

A student can be profited by closely studying trends. Anyone, and not merely a preacher, can be helped by examining, or testing, his faith and practice in their relation to his profession. But preachers of the Gospel of Christ should be especially careful at this point. Hence, tonight I call your attention to-

I. Trends Away From the American Restoration Movement.
  A. By the American Restoration Movement we refer to that movement which broke out in America about the turn of the nineteenth century. Several religious leaders and preachers in different parts of the country, sensing the evils of religious division and seeing how far from the New Testament pattern the denominations had drifted, began to call for unity. They urged that this could be done by abandoning human articles of faith, taking the Bible as the sole book of authority, and "speaking as the oracles of God." Most of these separate movements merged into one great appeal, and their mission was widely heralded as seeking to restore the New Testament pattern of the church. Their aims differed basically from those of the founders of the various Protestant sects. For example, Martin Luther, a Roman Catholic, originally fought merely to reform the corruptions of the Roman Catholic system, with never a thought to found-

ing another church or returning to the original, New Testament ground. But the Lutheran Church resulted. John Wesley, a member of the Church of England (Episcopalian), tried to reform that institution, injecting some warmth and feeling into the cold formalism and staid ceremonialism of that group. He made no effort to bring that denomination back to the Bible plan in its entirety. His efforts resulted in the Methodist Church.

But the men of the American Restoration Movement pleaded with religious people to do away with all sects; abolish all human creeds; surrender all practices of human origin; return to the New Testament pattern for the church; call Bible things by Bible names; in matters where God has legislated, to practice only that for which they could read a "thus saith the Lord;" and essentially and wholly restore the primitive, Christ-authorized, Holy Spirit-recorded, New Testament-written pattern for Christ's church. Their mission was to restore.

You young brethren, and other students, in our various Christian colleges are very properly being taught the history of that movement. There is a growing attention to that subject in the curricula of our colleges, and this emphasis comes none too soon. It is to be hoped that you will avail yourself of the opportunities to take courses in church history in general, and in the restoration movement in particular, and that you will pursue the subject after you finish college and all through your life. Then, as you preach the Gospel, you will help your audiences if you will frequently give them the historical facts in the case, doing considerable preaching and teaching on that subject. You will thus do a special service in combatting the popular fallacy of the Campbells having "founded this denomination," showing people that they did not originate this movement, and that we are no part of a denomination, but compose the New Testament church. By setting people straight on the facts of history, you will destroy many false impressions and influence people to think straight and see us in our true light. Of course, you can teach the New Testament picture of the church, if you never heard of any history after New Testament days. But you will find that you will have some useful tools with which to work if you can combine the teaching of the New Testament with the facts of

later history.
B. But please give heed to this caution.
   1. Those of us who do so much preaching on church history, and particularly the Restoration Movement, do not regard the pioneers in that later movement as our authority. For instance, when we quote from Walter Scott, Barton W. Stone, Thomas and Alexander Campbell, Moses E. Lard, J. W. McGarvey, and others, we never intend to make the impression that they are authorities. Please be careful on that point. A doctrine is not so just because those men believed it. It is true, of course, only if the New Testament teaches it. There are people who can misunderstand how we quote the Restoration pioneers if we are not exceedingly careful.
   2. There is, too, a sense in which it is altogether proper to move from them. They learned and progressed. So should we. For example, they learned that the Bible did not sustain "infant baptism," and they gave it up. For a few years, several of them did not understand that the "one baptism" of Eph. 4:5 was the "buried with Him by baptism...raised...to walk in newness of life" of Rom. 6:4. When they learned that, they gave up sprinkling and accepted baptism by a burial. So with other denominational practices. Those men were "coming out of the woods" of sectarian confusion, finding their way out of the wilderness of human doctrines into the clearing of "making all things according to the pattern" (Heb. 8:5) of the New Testament. We should move away from any of the men in that age who had not fully extricated themselves from such creedal shackles of human origin.
   3. But, there are three abiding attitudes for us to retain toward this movement.
      a. Their basic attitudes were correct. They sought to restore the New Testament pattern of the church by speaking "as the oracles of God." (1 Pet. 4:11) Certainly we can never leave that Gospel principle. Though those pioneers were wrong for a while on some of their practices, they had discovered the right principle by which to call people back to unity in Christ. Carpenters may be constructing a

building. For a while they may forsake—ignorantly or deliberately—the blueprints. They then will go far afield of the intent of the creator of the design for that house. The only way they can finally build that house according to the creator's desire is to stop where they are, go back to the blueprints, tear out anything not according to the specifications, and then build according to the plans as originally drawn. Now they have restored the basic and proper attitude, from which there should be no deviation. This was the attitude of the pioneers in the American Restoration Movement.

b. Further, their militant warfare was appropriate. They had to debate and fight for every inch of their ground. They were challenged on every side to give "a reason concerning the hope" which they proclaimed. People learned the truth in that way. Those who say that no one is convinced and converted by the proper kind of debates simply are ignorant of "the history of the case." This public contrasting of truth with error brought us to where we are today. I have personally known many leaders in the New Testament church, men who are elders, deacons, preachers, or teachers, who were strong denominationalists, but who learned their error in hearing a debate and accepted the truth as a result thereof. Our literature abounds with a multitude of others. Yes, there have been some poor debates, in which our men rushed in to tackle men beyond their ability to handle, or in which our men were either too lazy or too over-confident to prepare. There have been others where our men were just as offensive—and sometimes filthy—in their deportments as the sectarian debaters. But some ill-advised and poorly-conducted debates do not prove that they are all wrong, and they do not destroy the evidence of the many people, including whole congregations, who have been taught the truth by such a method. And this militant aggressiveness characterized all of their preaching. They "laid it on the line." They let people see the difference. They were not afraid to contrast the Gospel with human creeds,

Christ's New Testament church with human sects, and to let men see that they were preaching the one and only way to heaven. They left no one guessing as to what they meant, and they made no uncertain sound. They thought of the church as distinctive, and the Divine formula for unity as revealed in Eph. 4:4-6 was held before their audience, to the everlasting discomfort and frequent eruption of denominational preachers. We must not change our attitude as to their procedure being timely, nor say that it is out of date in our case.

c. There is also a proper and profitable use to be made of the restoration literature. A diligent study and full knowledge of the literature in this field will yield three important values.

   i. You will thereby be correctly informed in the history of the movement. That will give you accurate personal guidance. It will help you to correct false impressions in the public mind about these matters. For example, often we hear people say, "Thomas Campbell originated a creed for the Church of Christ, 'Where the Scriptures speak we speak, where the Scriptures are silent we are silent.'" A history of this movement will make you more efficient in answering that error. You will find that in 1809, as he and his associates were seeking a basis for Christian unity, he coined the phrase just quoted. But it was not a creed, or any part of it, of human origin. It was simply another way of saying precisely what you find the Holy Spirit said, through the apostle Peter, in 1 Pet. 4:11: "If any man speak, let him speak as the oracles of God." Campbell's motto, or expressed aim, was based on that Scripture. In lecture No. 3, in dealing with the preacher's library, I listed certain books describing the history of the American Restoration Movement, and in that data, you will find the story of how this expression was not a new creed of Campbell's, but his way of saying exactly what the New Testament already legislated. Again, you often hear people say, "Alexander Campbell started the

Church of Christ," and you can even read that in encyclopedias. But the history of this movement again shows that error: that men were preaching in various parts of the nation before Alexander Campbell even came here; that unity could be had only by laying aside human creeds and articles of faith, taking the Bible as containing our only law and all-sufficient rule of faith and practice; calling Bible things by Bible names, using only New Testament names for the church, etc.; that Thomas Campbell also came into this movement after it was started, and his son, Alexander, came to America in 1809, whereas these points were being urged in different parts of the country by the turn of that century, and even a little before; and that because of Alexander's superior scholastic attainment and personality drive, he came to be outstanding among the leaders, which gave him chief notice, and hence the errors of encyclopedias. And the literature will show in his writings, and that of others, that they were not starting a new church, but simply calling people back to the original pattern of the New Testament church. It is true that you can answer this false charge by the New Testament, but you can set the history of the movement in its true light before the public only as you know that history.

ii. We can also profit by learning their correct and incorrect positions, as contrasted with the New Testament.

iii. We can absorb their spirit of devotion to these unityproducing principles, their spirit of vigorously and militantly pressing the battle of truth against false ideas, their spirit of sacrifice, and their spirit of "having done all, to stand." For the foregoing reasons, I would urge you to accumulate a large number of books on this movement, as many as possible. No one book or set of books has all of the data. Some books are discovered to be in error on their data. You will, therefore, do well to acquire as many

books in this field as possible.
C. There is a drift, however, both from the principles and the spirit of the Restoration Movement. I here affirm that this drift takes three different forms.
   1. In distinctiveness as to the overall position. There is gradually growing a reluctance to make it clear that we are different. Too many preachers today are getting their sermons out of sectarian preachers' sermon books, with the result that you could listen to them a month and not identify their religious connection. Certainly, I agree that we should preach more than "first principles." But New Testament preaching, regardless of the subject, has a different ring from the sweet stand-for-nothingness of denominationalism. We are becoming more like the world as we grow in numbers, gather more people from the higher stations of life, increase in our material resources, and have more public attention focused upon ourselves. While we point with pride to our glowing and startling growth in numbers, property, and prestige, we are also growing in indulgence in light drinking, the modern dance, gambling around the bridge table and in other forms, as well as a general softening toward worldly practices. I believe that the most grave danger we face today is worldliness. We are losing our distinctiveness in many quarters as to Romans 12:2. Too many congregations become strong in numbers and other power, then settle down to comfortable complacency, teaching, acting, and living like the world around them. The discipline exercised in the average congregation of fifty or more years ago is rapidly becoming extinct. The pioneer churches demanded righteous and distinctive lives in their members, so that the world could see the difference between them and the world both in life and doctrine. Right at this point we certainly are drifting.
   2. There is a drift in militant aggressiveness, such as characterized the early days of the Restoration Movement in America, and which was also an attribute of the New Testament church. Some hesitate to affirm that we are the New Testament church, and that denominationalism is no part of it. The pioneers of this

Restoration Movement distinguished themselves for being a group of people who knew their position, and contended for it without apology or ambiguity. When you preach, do not blush to affirm that we are the church promised in Matt.16:18. No, you don't need to go around picking a scrap, nor to use a fighting, quarrelsome spirit in your preaching. I am not advocating that. But we can nevertheless drift from that original militant aggressiveness, if we are not most careful. Largeness of numbers, abundance of material resources, and wealth of power always produce complacency, an "at ease" attitude, if not closely watched.

3. The drift also is away from a study of the Bible. All of us were reared in an atmosphere of hearing people of the world freely compliment churches of Christ by speaking of how our people knew the Bible. It was one of our chief trademarks. Our preachers freely quoted Scriptures and cited the audiences to the references, "book, chapter, and verse," instead of merely saying that "the Bible says." The members in general were taught the book, knew it, and knew how to handle it. That was the very spirit of this movement. In spite of a drift away from this, these characteristics still distinguish our people, even if not in the same ratio or degree as a few decades back. We need to study that Book for all around, general purposes. And we need to study, so as to be equipped to contrast truth with error and to meet false doctrine, so that we may teach people out of the soul-destroying errors of sectarianism. Definite movements among us can be discerned, getting away from these early, and New Testament, principles and procedures.

Before leaving this part of our study, let me urge this, young men: you will do well to accumulate a considerable library of this Restoration Movement. Know that story. Absorb and retain its spirit. Hold to its basic principles. Of course, back of all this, we go to the New Testament. But the character who frowns upon your acquaintance with and presentation of the history of the American Restoration Movement should, to be consistent, never read any books of men, and never illustrate any point by such information. Don't allow any extremist among us to influence you to stick your head into the sand!

II. Four Critical Battlegrounds of Your Day.

Now we want to spend some major time in looking over four critical battlegrounds of your day. (Author's note—Only the first two of these "critical battlegrounds" were discussed under separate headings in the lectures at Central Christian College, while the third one was added in this form in the lecture at David Lipscomb College. However, some of the material for the third and fourth was scattered through the speeches in the first engagement. And some of the material for the fourth was liberally spread through the lectures at DLC. It was thought best in the book to arrange all of the points in this field of study under these four separate headings.)

There are other critical battlegrounds. There are other issues, in addition to those named under these four headings. Under no circumstances would I leave you under the impression that I think you need be concerned only about Modernism, Roman Catholicism, Extremism, and Worldliness, which are here to be discussed. We are not forgetting that we have stressed in these lectures that one special pitfall for a Gospel preacher is that of going to seed in crusading for a single issue. So, we certainly are not urging your exclusive attention to these four issues. The point is, rather, that these four critical battlegrounds are facing the church in a very special way, and we should prepare ourselves to face them in the best way. An army defending a given city will make special efforts to defend a point of heavy attack. That is the thought I have here in mind.

    A. There is the battleground of Modernism. Among other things, modernism denies the verbal inspiration of the Bible, as affirmed in 1 Cor. 2:12-13. It denies Gen. 1:1 as to origin of the universe and man. It denies Rom. 5:12 as to sin. It denies Matt. 1:18-25 as to the Sonship of Jesus Christ. It denies Rom. 3:23-25 as to sin and redemption. It denies Acts 17:30-31 as to the final judgment, presided over by Christ as our Judge. It denies Matt. 25:46 as to final destiny. Here, and at other points attacked by modernism, we are going to have to make special preparation and effort. In addition to studying the Bible diligently along these lines, and stressing such points in your preaching and teaching, you should equip yourself with the best books in this field.

I do not mean, however, that we are to "go to seed" or make hobbies of these matters. Nor is it my intention to leave the impression that we should leave other battlefields, such as the "seven ones" of Eph. 4:4-6, baptism for the remission of sins (Acts 2:38), the singing in worship of 1 Cor. 14:15, 23, and the sin of mechanical instrumentation in worship. I do not mean that we are to tone down on opposition to all false systems, including the heresy of millennialism, which we have fought for years. But we naturally mass our forces at particular points of attack, while not going to sleep at other points to be guarded. Modernism is making a major attack today at the points here named. It should receive special attention. Collect good literature on the subject. Study the Bible, and in conversation, class, and pulpit, contrast this heresy with what the Bible says and why we should believe what the Bible says on these subjects. Actually, modernism furnishes you an ideal chance to show that it is the natural result of present-day denominationalism.

B. There is the critical battleground of Roman Catholicism.
   1. Roman Catholicism is making a big play for America, trying to gain here what she is rapidly losing in Europe.
   2. She is practicing deliberate deception in two major ways.
      a. In calling for religious liberty in America, but denying it in Italy and in any other country which she controls.
      b. In advertising principles as if they were doctrines of Roman Catholicism, which are flatly opposite to their official doctrine as on record and to the proven practice. For example, in publishing ads claiming that the Roman Catholic Church believes in religious liberty, she willfully deceives, in view of her official doctrine that when she can control a government, that government is to proclaim Roman Catholicism the state religion and forbid other religions the right to propagate their ideas. (See Catholic Principles Of Politics, by Ryan and Boland, 1950 printing, pages 316, 317.)
   3. Roman Catholicism has a big advantage in America.
      a. There is her use of force and fear.

b. America has been noted for religious liberty and tolerance. Hence, in the days when Catholics were few in this country, Americans showed their toleration by protecting Roman Catholicism against persecutors. Now that Roman Catholicism has multiplied, she thrives on this advantage of the American attitude.
c. There aids her, too, the stand-for-nothing policy of the Protestant sects. Most of them are afraid to oppose her, and the same spirit is taking hold of government. If you will watch the "brotherhood forums," under various names in the communities of the nations, where the speakers or panelists will be a Catholic priest, a Jewish rabbi, and a Protestant clergyman, you will notice that the Protestant preacher will always fail to take a positive position on any point of controversy, but will so "love everybody with toleration" that any way to heaven is satisfactory with him—that the Catholic and Jew will stand by his side in heaven, according to him! If he doesn't say that, he leaves that impression, and no one gets the idea that the differences make any difference. But you never find a Catholic priest making any concession to the Protestants in point of conviction. Further, occasionally you find a public school, as did our Shades Valley High School in Homewood recently, will use a Catholic priest as the speaker in commencement exercises—but where do you ever find a Catholic school exposing their students to a Protestant clergyman under the same circumstances? Any informed Christian knows of numbers of ways in which Protestant denominations make concessions to Roman Catholicism, and how even various units of government allow the Roman Catholic Church to get away with practices not allowed to others.
4. Roman Catholicism is a twin threat with Communism. They are parallel evils. They partake of the same nature, and are basically identical in spirit.
   a. Both are governed by the final authority of one man—though, since the death of Stalin, Communism seems to have top authority divided among a few. The principle of authority of the two forces,

however, is the same. The only reason that Communism now perhaps does not have one absolute dictator, as was Stalin, is only because no one man among them seems to have that much power. Under both Roman Catholicism and Russian Communism (identical initials for each system) the individual has no liberty except such as the dictator allows. The same is true of opposition parties—religious and political.
   b. Both use force to enforce their authority.
   c. Both would deny all liberty to all who oppose. As to Roman Catholicism, in this lecture, under point 2 of this major subdivision B, I cited you to the authoritative, official statement of that denomination to that effect, in the book Catholic Principles Of Politics, by Ryan and Boland, 1950 printing, pages 316-317. As to Russian Communism, her history of the past few years, in ruthlessly running over smaller European countries, proves that to be her position. Hungary, for example, is a "shining" example.
   d. Both contradict the revealed Word of God, as found in the Bible. In the final analysis, there is no difference in the two systems.
5. Roman Catholicism's attack on the Gospel in Italy was a high tribute to the strength of the Gospel of Christ and Catholicism's fear of the people hearing it. She does not wage the same fight on other religious groups in Italy.
6. So, study her doctrines in her authoritative works.
7. Be sure you know her doctrines, and that you correctly represent her.
8. Then, diligently teach all congregations and individuals as much as you can of her errors.
9. Especially warn young people against marrying Catholics, and show them what such marriages will bring upon themselves and their children.
10. In view of the compromising position of the Protestant sects, of the growing power of Catholicism, and of the fact that Roman Catholicism has something definite to offer, Gospel preachers are going to find in the immediate years to come more of a challenge from that source than from any other group in

America. By the same token, let Roman Catholicism find its principal challenge coming from churches of Christ.
C. There is the critical battleground of Radicalism, Extremism. During the past few years, this problem has developed within ourselves. And it has gained greater momentum, as the Herald Of Truth has been maintained—a national broadcast of the Gospel, over approximately 800 radio stations, with the Highland Ave. church, in Abilene, TX, putting this program on, assisted by hundreds of congregations and many individuals, said program now being in its eighth year. Now, as I talk to you about extremism, about radicalism, I am taking into account that it would be "politically expedient" to say nothing along this line. And, as these lectures are written in permanent form in a book, I know full well that to express my convictions on these issues will arouse some opposition and close the door to sale of the book in some quarters. Many men, wanting to sell a book, would sidestep any controversial issues. If I know my own heart, I can say that I am more interested in whatever influence I and the book may have for the right side of issues than in the sale of the book. After all, a man is complimented by his enemies as much as by his friends. And it is my prayer, young brethren, that, as you carve your place as a Gospel preacher, you may be correctly known for not fearing to state your convictions, instead of being the opportunist trying to stand in with everything and against nothing. After all, if you state no convictions, you have no convictions.
1. By radicalism, or extremism, I mean: the practice of pressing true principles to extreme, to radical, and/or to untrue conclusions. When people indulge in this practice, they also begin to create erroneous principles. But, generally, the error here comes about more from those who press true principles to extreme conclusions. A group of extremists can keep up such a fight in behalf of their positions that in course of time they will mislead some very sincere and intelligent people. They always have a sympathetic ear among us when they cry out against the dangers of departure, of large errors coming from small beginnings, for we always have stressed that in

our preaching. We should. This being very properly one of the more prominent features of our preaching, it is more easy for us, unless we are exceedingly careful, to be led into these extreme positions of opposing some worthwhile projects purely because of the danger of departure. An extreme pressing of a true principle right here can lead us into opposition against any and every good work. Suppose we examine how this extremism is manifesting itself in the fight over congregational cooperation in general and the Herald of Truth radio network broadcast in particular.

A few years ago, a weekly religious paper among us started this agitation. Hardly has an issue been printed without one or several articles being printed on these issues. The attacks have been savage, the spirit caustic, and the attitude almost uniform that all who disagree with them are simply trying to line up with the popular side. Their theme has constantly been that they are crusading for soundness, and they have sold many readers on the notion that if the church is saved from complete apostasy, it will be because of their fight. They represent themselves as the only ones "sound in the faith," only their paper— plus the very few small ones that support them, only the one college among us, which up to this moment is committed through its administration and dominant part of its board, to the same position. (And we trust that that school may yet be saved from this radicalism.) They represent themselves as the only honest ones. Only they are moved by conviction. In practically every case of there being any public announcement of the several preachers who have abandoned their position, they describe those making the changes as not sincere, moved only by the desire to be on the "popular bandwagon" and not having any real conviction. This is standard, uniform procedure with them in dealing with those who oppose in their paper articles and sermons. It doesn't seem to occur to them that other preachers, writers, elders, teachers, papers, and colleges can be just as sincere in convictions as they represent themselves as being. This is a disease, deplorable, and leading their writers in most cases to completely misrepresent those from whom they differ. Even the spirit of such a movement should be repugnant to people enough to make them suspicious of the merit even of their position. A number of brethren, including some with whom I have been closely associated, have been persuaded that their position is right. I certainly believe that most of the people over the country committed to these views are sincere. But I believe that they have taken some New Testament principles and pressed them to extreme positions. In fact, it is my conviction that they have done exactly what the "anti-Sunday school" people have done.

a. The anti-Lord's-Day-Bible-classes people have taken the true New Testament principle that we should "make all things according to the pattern," (Heb. 8:5) and claimed that the Lord's Day Bible classes as practiced by us violate that rule. They claim that these classes are exactly in the same position as mechanical instruments of music in worship, that such a class system is an innovation. Their objection to the classes is on the ground that "there is no New Testament example of such classes on the Lord's Day." Well, we admit that we find no example in the New Testament of a church setting aside a time for a number of classes just before the observance of the Lord's Supper. But we insist that the absence of such an example does not prove that the practice violates the New Testament permission. We understand fully how we justify our practice. For example, we point to the principle of "teach all nations" in the Great Commission of Matt. 28:19, insisting that "go" and "teach" are general terms, whereas the "singing" of Eph. 5:19 and Col. 3:16 is a specific term; that the going and teaching are thus left to our judgment, as long as they do not contradict other specified New Testament principles, but that the music in worship is specified, forbidding other music. Instead of adding something to the Lord's Day assembly worship, as is charged, we have these various Bible classes before the assembly worship. They are not, then, added to the worship. The "anti's," who talk so "soundly" about our departing from the pattern because we find no example of such, should cease having a song leader in their worship. We have no example of such a song leader in the New Testament. Yet we agree with them when they justify the use of a song leader. When they justify that, however, they are defending a practice in worship for which they find no example. It is possible, then, to press this "no example" argument to a radical extreme. That is precisely what they do in objecting to the Bible classes.

b. Again, the Carl Ketcherside-Leroy Garrett groups yell loudly that there is no example of a New Testament church employing a preacher with a church for a definite time at a stated salary, and that thus our practice is wrong. We concede that there is no such example of that complete case. We find New Testament preachers with churches, giving full time to the work and being supported. For more detailed arguments on this, look back to the first lecture in this series. Though we find no case of a preacher drawing a stated salary for a definite time, we know how we justify the practice within New Testament permission, and the absence of the example does not deny the right for the practice.

c. Now, those who oppose Herald of Truth and any such form of congregational cooperation, have—quite sincerely in most cases—"gone to seed" in using this "no example" argument. Every argument which they make is made by the anti-classes and anti-fulltimepreacher group. (I heard a man preaching in Birmingham since these lectures, who went down the line on this argument opposing Herald of Truth. As he preached on having nothing except what the pattern calls for, he even went to the extreme of classifying having trustees for church property in the same category. That shows how far a radical, extreme principle will drive folks.) As a matter of fact, they are basically and fundamentally so similar that they should all join hands. I do not doubt that the more extreme among them will do just exactly that.

They go strong on the argument that "there is no example of a large number of congregations contributing to one church to preach the Gospel in a given area." But before you are deceived by that line of reasoning, be sure that you are not driven to extremism by extreme pressing of a true principle. And mark this: when brethren do this, they wind up taking positions or urging principles that are not true. Press a true principle to an untrue extreme, and you will then manufacture untrue principles.

For example, they argue that when Homewood church, Birmingham, with which I labor, sends money to Highland church in Abilene, TX, to help support our national Gospel broadcast, the Herald of Truth, our congregational autonomy (independence) is violated. On the contrary, we exercise that congregational independence by deciding to send that money, by earmarking it to be spent for a specific purpose. The Highland church exercises its independence by deciding to invite churches to assist, by accepting the money, and by carrying on the program with money sent for that purpose. The autonomy of no church is violated. Highland church contracts for the program and can terminate the program when thought best. But we understand that when we send our money and send it with that knowledge. Just where has any contributing church, including Highland, lost its autonomy? Only in the charges of those who continue to make these false charges and make good brethren believe such to be true.

Then they charge that Highland church is turned into a missionary society, and that contributing churches are sending their money to such an organization. Wrong. The difference is this: a missionary society is a board of men, members of various congregations, over the country, banded into an organization outside of and separate and apart from a congregation to do the work of the church, in competition with the church. But Highland church is not such an organization, but is a congregation under the oversight of its elders, according to New Testament authorization. (Acts 20:17, 28; 14:23) So, in supporting this great program of blanketing our nation, and many adjacent nations, with the Gospel, you are not sending money to a missionary society, but to a congregation.

Then, some of them charge that Herald of Truth is separate from the church because for it, Highland church, in Abilene, TX, has a separate bank account, a separate treasurer, and with one elder delegated to supervise it. They seem to forget that congregations often employ this practice for special projects. For example, when the Homewood congregation launched a project looking ultimately to the building of our second and "main" building, we created a separate building fund account and with one brother in charge of that fund. That money was kept separate from our general fund, and the general fund treasurer never touched a dime of it. That wasn't because we lacked confidence in our general fund treasurer. On the contrary, his job was a big one, and this treasureship for the building fund was to be a big one. Further, to keep the two separate not only spread work among the treasurers, instead of overloading one, but it simplified bookkeeping. Too, we kept before the people that every penny which went into the building fund would go for that purpose and could be spent for nothing else. That helped to establish confidence and increased incentive. Only after the building was finished and duly financed did we abolish the separate fund and vacate the office of a separate building fund treasurer. While we had that plan, did that mean that our building fund was separate from the Homewood church? That our treasurer for that fund was separate? Did that mean that such fund constituted a separate organization? That is all that the separate Herald of Truth fund in Highland church operation means. The fact that one elder is appointed to supervise it does not mean he is apart from the other elders, as one Birmingham preacher "interpreted" a letter from him to mean, but simply, as this elder later explained in more places than one, that he was to handle contacts and relations with the contributing congregations, so that they may look to one particular elder to whom to address interested inquiries, and to have one elder responsible for that work as others were for other tasks. The foregoing Homewood practice has been standard with congregations, and it is not questioned in any quarter.

Then they charge that this is a super organization of churches, and that is not even a remote kin to the truth. There simply is no organization, except each separate congregation. Homewood church is a contributing church, but we have our own local, separate congregation, under the oversight of our elders, as the elders are assisted by our deacons, and we are not joined to Highland church in any organizational way. Neither are we connected with any other contributing congregation. Neither is Highland church connected with us. Some talk much about "The Church Universal," but no one is promoting such, no one is practicing such, and nothing being done even tends in that direction. Highland church is not doing our work for us, as they charge. We are carrying on our own program, and assisting Highland with a program which those brethren found themselves able to carry on in part, but for which they need help in maintaining in its entirety. We agree with all of the great preaching being done on respecting the New Testament plan of organization and work, but deny that congregational cooperation as we practice it either violates the principle or is a step in that direction.

We support Herald of Truth on the principles of the church being "the pillar and ground of the truth" (1 Tim. 3:14-15); the great commission charging us with the duty of "teaching all nations" (Matt. 28:19); the authority of the congregation so to do in any way not violating revealed New Testament laws; the right of the congregation to contribute money for the preaching of the Gospel as long as no organization unknown to the New Testament pattern is set up, as long as there is no intercongregational organization, and we deny that any New Testament law is violated by Herald of Truth.

If you have observed the increasing momentum and bitterness of this fight in the paper which is leading it, you see why I list this Radicalism, or Extremism, as one of the critical battlegrounds facing you. But the reason becomes more obvious and the possible future more ominous when you look a little further. Those opposing Herald of Truth are arguing that the set-up is a missionary society; that we who support it are in exactly the same position as those who introduced the missionary society among us in the 19th century; and that we who support Herald of Truth are as guilty of driving the wedge that is splitting the church as were the society engineers in 1849. Not all of the anti-Herald of Truth people are arguing this, but their more active writers and debaters are thus arguing. The rest of them will eventually come to it, unless they see the enormity of their folly and return to more sensible ground. If this argument be true, those opposing Herald of Truth should not fellowship those of us supporting it. We do not support or fellowship the churches which support the missionary society. We do not employ, support, or fellowship preachers who stand with that crowd. If congregational cooperation as practiced by us today, in Herald of Truth and other features of our evangelistic work, is parallel with the missionary society, then those who oppose that work should not fellowship us. That is the step the anti-Sunday school people took. It is the result of the Ketcherside-Garrett movements. It logically follows that it must inevitably be the position of the anticongregational-cooperation-as-per-Herald-of-Truth people. Is that what they want? As to their leaders, I am persuaded that this is what they are driving for, and there they will land. As one example of this, in the Gospel Guardian, which has spearheaded the attacks against Herald of Truth, orphan homes, etc., issue of Sept. 5, 1957, there appeared a report from one of the Birmingham preachers of that persuasion, informing the readers that fellowship "with the institutional crowd" was gradually being broken and endorsing this attitude on the part of the anti-orphan home, anti-Herald of Truth groups. Another Birmingham preacher admitted to me that the situation was coming to that. Of course, we who support these works have no intention of breaking fellowship with people simply because they cannot conscientiously support orphan homes or congregational cooperation such as Herald of Truth. While we do not agree with their judgment, we recognize that as their privilege and have no desire to force these matters upon them. What we oppose is their forcing their objections to such on the brotherhood, as far as they are able, and binding these ideas as laws. Then it is that we must publicly and firmly oppose that which becomes a hobby and cause of division. And the foregoing report is just one of the many straws showing which way the wind is blowing, that their leaders intend to make these matters a test of fellowship whenever they can drum up enough strength in a given place. In Mississippi, a congregation was established from an old one. The new one claimed that these issues had nothing to do with the creation of the new church. They accepted the services of a preacher who did oppose orphanages and Herald of Truth, and who was supported by an Alabama church which was most aggressive in this same opposition. When this preacher went through a prolonged course of study and prayer and decided that he had been in error on both counts, he sent a statement to that effect to the Gospel Advocate. The day after that statement appeared in the paper, this church—which had previously claimed these issues were not involved in its program—fired the preacher as of the following day! Their "official organ" does not tell of these scenes occurring over the nation. The brotherhood needs to know where the leaders of these hobbies are headed. The tragedy is that, in addition to the more radical leaders, they will deceive and lead off many good brethren. But I am persuaded that as more brethren see the unavoidable end to their position, they will call a halt before they reap the whirlwind, for they will see the senseless and deplorable results of their radical extremism. This is where you are going to have to make up your mind as to where you stand, and I appeal to you to think a long time before being stampeded into extremism by a radical doctrine that crusades under the name of keeping the church sound, but is actually heading into the same results as those of the anti-Sunday school and Ketcherside-Garrett groups.

There are preachers who do not agree with the extremists, but who will not state their convictions, for they do not want to arouse the bitter antagonism of the more extreme ones, lest doors be closed to meetings and other work. But you have to pay a price for conviction. At the same time, you can keep in mind that by far the overwhelming number of people in the extreme camps are entirely sincere, and have simply been misled. You can treat them in that spirit and work for the peace and unity of the church, without yielding any ground to error.

D. There is the critical battleground of Worldliness. My considered judgment, my profound conviction is that THIS is THE MOST CRITICAL ISSUE before the church. The battle here has been shaping up with growing momentum. Companies of soldiers among us have surrendered, and there is reason to look with alarm.
   1. Before urging you to take any attitude toward worldliness, let us see first exactly what it is. Now, worldliness is being like the world. So, what does the Bible mean by the word world or being like the world? There is too much loose talking about the subject, and sometimes men are too prone to label something as in that category just because it does not meet with their personal approval. A more detailed study is recommended just here. You will find much

valuable material on the use of the word world in the Bible by consulting Bible encyclopedias, among the best of which I would recommend for this study is The International Standard Bible Encyclopedia article on "World," Vol. 5, pages 3108-9. I have carefully checked this data with the Biblical passages and believe the material to be accurate and most helpful.

Among the many words in the original languages of the Bible from which the English word world is drawn, only 3 are here mentioned. First, there is the Old Testament word Tebhel (English spelling), meaning simply "globe, man's material dwelling place," as in Psa. 90:1-2. Second, there is the New Testament Greek Kosmos. Its meaning varies. Sometimes it is "earthly possessions," as in Matt. 16:26; or "earth and man as the creation of the Word," as in John 1:10; or "mankind as alienated by sin from God," as also in John 1:10. Third, there is the New Testament Greek Aion, meaning "age" or "ages." Sometimes it will be: time extended, on and on, as in Eph. 3:21. Sometimes, it will be a particular age, as in Luke 20:35. "Then, in view of the moral contents of the present state of things, it freely passes into the thought of forces and influences tending against faith and holiness, e.g., 2 Cor. 4:4." (ISBE, Vol. 5, page 3109) This latter sense is the way I use it in this lecture, and is the sense in which the New Testament condemns worldliness.

Scriptures showing the Worldly principle contrary to the good of the church as such are 1 John 2:15-16; Gal. 1:4; Eph. 2:1-2; 2 Cor. 6:14-7:1; Titus 2:11-12; and Rom. 12:2. Thus the church's one persistent, continuous effort is to "be not conformed to this world: but be ye transformed by the renewing of your mind..." Some Bible "specifics" of this worldly principle are found in such Scriptures as Gal. 5:19-21 and 1 Cor. 6:9-10.

Now, notice some modern exhibitions of this worldly principle.

a. Forsaking of the assembly when preferred, in violation of Heb. 10:25 and Matt. 6:33.
b. Regularity of assembly attendance, but not contributing of our money to the home church with regularity on the first day of the week: whether present or absent (1 Cor. 16:2); according to

planned or purposed amounts set aside for the Lord and not stolen from Him just because we had to be absent (2 Cor. 9:7); and according to sacrifice (Lk. 9:23).

c. Vulgar speech, including such jokes, or laughing at such, instead of reproving such. (Eph. 5:3-4)
d. Loose marriage standards, ending in divorce and remarriage, without the one New Testament permission (Matt. 19:3-9), with adultery, and being sealed off from heaven. (1 Cor. 6:9-10)
e. Drinking of intoxicating beverages. Drunkenness shuts off from heaven. (Gal. 5:19-21) The power of strong drink on the average person and the New Testament doctrine of responsibility for our influence (1 Cor. 8) will keep any Christian from even the "lightest" or social drinking.
f. Gambling's growing power in blighting incomes and homes justifies you in putting the label of worldliness on it, in view of its evil fruit (Matt. 7:20) and Christian responsibility for influence.
g. Vulgar literature justifies the label on the very face of it, for it defies all Bible passages bearing on purity of mind ("For as he thinketh within himself, so is he"—Prov. 23:7), and one reading that literature or feasting on such pictures is simply feeding on that which is impure.
h. The same goes for the indecent dress of women and men in public. Every time a "Christian" woman parades in public in shorts—and the shorter some of them get, the better some women seem to prefer them—she violates"...that women adorn themselves in modest apparel." (1 Tim. 2:9) Men can get just as vulgar in the neighborhood, stores, parks, etc. The very public exhibition of the body tends to make men have less respect for women and chastity, and it is most difficult for me to see how any woman who defends this near-nudity in public can sincerely believe that such is in the interest of public morals.
i. The modern dance is basically worldly. It appeals to the fleshly contact between the sexes, as proved by the fact that it would die if men were forced to dance only with men and women only

with women. Further, while there are varying "positions" on the dance floor, if a man walked up to a woman on the street and took her in the position that is customary at the modern dance, there would be criticism and, sometimes, trouble. Yet, in the dance such is fine! Surely there are some good people morally who dance, but the basis of the dance is wrong morally and tends in that direction. I have observed that in the average case, the person who takes a growing interest in the dance takes a lessening interest in spirituality and the church, and "by their fruits ye shall know them." (Matt. 7:20) And those who dance certainly damage, or destroy, their influence for good in the church. That is in violation of the principle of 1 Cor. 8. There are well-known books containing the testimony of former dancing instructors and matrons of homes for fallen girls who testify that the women testify that the dance was the start of their downfall. And yet gullible people are simple enough to deny its danger. That is because they do not WANT to believe the evidence. Usually, they are more concerned with popularity, and that is the big argument used for the modern dance. They need to believe the principle of Gal. 1:10.

j. We are convinced that the trend of our women to ape the men in smoking is purely of the world, conforming to the world. Such is cheapening them in the public eye. And the war over the potential power of cigarette tobacco is enough to make women leave it alone, unless they are heedless to danger. 1 Thess. 5:22 will help the sincere ones among them.

k. Marrying those not members of the New Testament church is one of the most damaging of worldly evils. Israel of the Old Testament was a type of the church of the New Testament. Yet Israel was flatly forbidden marrying out of the Israelite religion because of the danger of the Israelite so married compromising. If dangerous for Israel, who would deny the danger for the church? Rarely do you find a Christian marrying one out of the church but that the Christian, though very faithful, will compromise here and there. It confuses children, sets a barrier in the home, and does everything against the spirituality of the church that such marriages in the Old Testament did for Israel.

2. Your parents and the older preachers among us can easily remember when this country in general, and churches of Christ in particular, had much higher standards of conduct than now. There was a more definite line of distinctiveness in character between the world and the church. Even the denominations lived on a much higher plane. Discipline was exercised by the congregations of Christ. Dancing and drinking of whiskey, wine, and beer, along with gambling, were not tolerated among the members of the church. Parents exercised discipline in the home. Preachers sounded a clear, unmistakable note along these lines. Elders demanded and supported such teaching. Teachers were not allowed in classes who transgressed at these points, nor were elders, deacons, and preachers maintained who wavered here. There were exceptions, of course, and such exceptions caused reverberations and disturbances that turned the spotlight upon them, and they were held up as examples to be abhorred by others.

3. But look at the changing scene. There are still multitudes of churches, preachers, elders, deacons, teachers, and members in general who are as sound as sound can be on these points. But there has been a definite lowering of standards. Hardly anyone questions, in the first place, that the morals of the country have deteriorated. The movies, theaters, magazines, papers, and television get away with scenes, remarks, and writing that would not have been even thought of in any public medium just a few generations ago. The sects have moved from ancient belief in the inspiration of the Bible, and over 98 per cent of their theological seminaries have gone to Modernism, in varying and growing degrees. They have degenerated in their convictions on final judgment, hell, sin, and obedience. That necessarily means a lowering of the moral standards. Both Catholic

and Protestant groups, including many Disciples or Christian churches, have given the modern dance the sheltering sponsorship of their churches. Ditto gambling devices. Our public schools are exerting tremendous and growing efforts to commit our young people to the modern dance. There are devout, high-type school teachers and administrators, but their number is decreasing and the whole spirit of the school system is to inculcate worldly standards of conduct contrary to the basic position of religion and school of generations ago. This naturally comes with the gradual seeping into our school books the ideas that the Bible is not inspired and that the Genesis account of creation is false. Of necessity, when they depart from the teaching of the Bible as to creation and authority, there will be a departure from the moral standards of the Bible. So, churches of Christ live in a country that has degenerated in morals, among religious groups who have departed from former high standards, and attend schools that are fully imbibing the spirit of the age and area.

4. All of that has had a withering, blighting influence upon the church. There are few congregations where there are not many, or at least a few, who go in for the dancing, gambling around the bridge table and in other forms, and drinking—either "heavy" or "light." It is becoming increasingly difficult to look at a crowd of people and know by either their dress, speech, conduct, or where they go the ones who are members of the church of the Lord and those who are out in the world. In public places, you will find many "Christian" women wearing just as little clothing as the briefest-clad of the world. As they have absorbed so much of the spirit of the world, you can find more of them known for coarseness and even profanity of speech, matching the hardened and "manly" men in that respect. There is a tendency on the part of some in mixed groups to have a freedom of speech and even touch that is no compliment to the standards and morals of our people. Hardly anyone denies that an increasing number of women in the church are no different from those of the world in their smoking habits, and apparently they

are seeking to make up for lost time in matching the men in this respect. It is a frequent occurrence to find congregations with a large number of people divorced and remarried—and the elders derelict in their duties as shepherds in having not the slightest idea if they have Bible grounds for divorce and remarriage (as in Matt. 19:9) or not. Every argument that elders can make today for not inquiring into the scripturalness of divorce in the congregations which they oversee could have been made in the case of the man living in adultery in the Corinthian church. (1 Cor. 5) But Paul reproved the church for closing its eyes, permitting it, and demanded a public withdrawal of fellowship. (See vs. 4-5) But it is a mark of worldliness that elders, preachers, and others argue against the Holy Spirit in this Scripture. There are preachers who have the widespread reputation among us of saying nothing against those worldly evils. Some will speak out against such in congregations where such preaching is desired and "safe," but will say nothing where such will be unpopular. There are preachers who will say privately that they are against such worldliness, and may do a little, occasional, faint preaching on the subject that would give a slight suspicion that they would prefer that people refrain from such blighting practices. But their preaching along this line is so seldom and weak that the worldly members gravitate in that direction and remain in such congregations with comfort. You can go to congregations and find that the pulpit and eldership have completely abandoned all opposition to such, where the children of preachers, elders, deacons, and teachers dance, drink, and gamble. You can preach against such in a meeting and use the best spirit and most careful language—and close the door against ever being called there for a meeting. Parents will insist that they oppose their children engaging in the modern dance, and even talk to them some about it; but they allow them to do so, excusing their weakness and backboneless action by saying, "we just can't forbid them." That attitude has been absorbed from the general spirit of the age. Discipline has just about broken down in both

school and home. Some good preachers have grown discouraged and surrendered, figuring that there is no way to stop the worldly trend.
5. Right here you will do well to gird yourself for battle. To me, this is THE CRISIS before the church. Any -ism among us needs to be held up to the light for full inspection. Premillennialism needs to be fought with vigor and never put on the shelf as a "dead issue." It will always pose a devastating threat. But worldliness, in my sincere judgment, poses a greater threat against us right now than any one issue. There has been such a rapid drift. Less is being said on the subject. Many of those who spend their time warring over institutionalism, cooperation, etc., are as silent as the grave on this growing menace. We can ride hobbies and push extremes, and at the same time let the church be engulfed by the cunning of the appeal of worldliness. That is precisely what is going on among us. Young brethren, we had best awake.
6. Don't spend all of your time preaching on this—or any—subject. But meet this attack where it is being aimed. Arm yourself with Scriptures showing the distinctiveness between the church and world, such as Rom. 12:1-2; 2 Cor. 6:14-7:1; and 1 John 2:15-17. Show the inherent, natural evil of these worldly practices, as well as their evil fruit, and apply Matt. 7:20. Stress the damage to influence, and show the obligation to respect such. (1 Cor. 8 and 10:31-33) Call attention to the fact that the average member of the church who is soft, for example, upon dancing, is soft on any worldly evil. And the worldly elements will stand together when any issue comes up in the church along that line. I repeat: he who is soft on one of these worldly practices is generally soft on all of them. Point out the fact that those who dance, drink, and gamble will generally take a lessening interest in the work of the Lord and a growing interest in such indulgencies.
7. The history of the case is that, as the church grows larger, has more prominence, and adds more material resources, and as the members find themselves in higher stations among people of the world, then a softening influence sets in, and we grow more like

the world. He who denies this, if he is sincere in his denial, proves himself ignorant of the data on record in the New Testament and in history since the days of the New Testament.

Now we are growing by leaps and bounds. We are making more of an impact upon the world. But it must be admitted that in the average case, the church that can point to its age, greater size, buildings, and prominence will find the withering influence of worldliness wielding its blighting influence. We cannot make laws on the size of churches and buildings where God has not legislated, and we are not to indict all churches of size as thus guilty. We must take the privileges of growth—for, after all, we want to convert multitudes—and material power as a challenge, and especially prepare ourselves so as not to be "conformed to the world." Here, to me, is a critical battleground, and the most critical one, facing us today.

CHAPTER 15
OPPORTUNISTS AND DISCOURAGEMENTS

In this final talk on the general theme of the day-by-day mechanics of doing the work of a Gospel preacher, we will give attention to Opportunists and Discouragements. They blight the work of preachers and congregations. This series of lectures would not be complete unless we gave special and considerable attention to these problems. And this is the logical place to consider them.

I. **Opportunists.**
   A. First, let's make it quite clear as to what we mean by this term. Merriam-Webster Unabridged Dictionary gives this definition of an opportunist: "One who follows the art, policy, or practice of taking advantage, as in politics, of opportunities or circumstances, or often, of seeking immediate advantage with little regard for principles or ultimate consequences." Opportunists in all walks of life—including preachers—are quite plentiful. In the beginning of your work as a Gospel preacher, you need to set the pattern of your life against such characteristics. Actually, it should have been so set years before you began preaching. But, if you are a little inclined toward opportunism in preaching, now is the time to take stock and entirely cleanse yourself from your political maneuvering.
   B. In order to steel and protect himself against this spirit

of opportunism, a Gospel preacher needs to fill himself with a plentiful supply of conviction as taught in the Bible, "And as these went their way, Jesus began to say unto the multitudes concerning John, 'What went ye out into the wilderness to behold? A reed shaken with the wind?'" (Matt 11:7) John did not bend to the popular breeze in any such fickle and weak fashion. The illustration our Lord had in mind was that of the wind bending the reed in any direction "desired" by the wind. Men are often like that. Whatever the public wants, that is what they give the public. But John was just the opposite. Instead of consulting the popular or reigning wish in his selection and treatment of topics, he inquired as to the desires of his God, and faithfully performed the same. Here our Lord gave one of the most impressive lessons on a public man having some convictions and standing by them.

You need right here, however, to make a distinction between stubbornness in matters where the Lord has not legislated, and unyielding loyalty to what God has said. Many preachers confuse the two, putting the second in place of the first, and doing much unnecessary damage. The latter—unyielding loyalty to what God has said—is what Christ here recommended, "Woe unto you, when all men shall speak well of you! For in the same manner did their fathers to the false prophets." (Lk. 6:26) Our Lord did not in this passage disparage our living so as to command the respect of people, but He condemned the opportunist, who preaches what people want, doing so to feather his own nest, regardless of the ultimate consequences upon the souls of men. A most excellent illustration of this text is 1 Kings 22, where about 400 opportunist prophets told Ahab and Jehoshaphat that God would bless them in a proposed military expedition. They claimed to have consulted God, but they lied. They testified falsely because they knew that such testimony was what their employer-king wanted to hear. But one prophet, Micaiah, told them the opposite, the truth. It was one prophet teaching the truth versus 400 reeds shaken by the wind, because they wanted to stand in with their employer. They were willing to make an impression that would please their master and help them materially, at the expense of defying God and distorting truth. Actually, their temporary gain turned into an ultimate and permanent loss. You can easily imagine what sort of preachers these prophets would be today. Other splendid scriptural pictures of this point are Isa. 30:8-14; Acts 4:18-31; and Eph. 6:13.

C. Next, let us notice some marks of an opportunist, or a "reed shaken with the wind." He is not difficult to spot.
   1. He evades taking a stand on points of doctrine in certain places. If some members of prominence object to preaching against millennialism, he evades any clear stand on that issue. If some object to opposition from the pulpit to worldliness, and being specific about such matters, he may mildly preach against worldliness, but will go lightly on telling what it is. Especially will that be true if the sons and daughters of some of the "leading'" members dance, drink, gamble, live in adultery, etc. If he lives in a city where those opposing churches contributing to orphan homes and congregational cooperation such as Herald of Truth are sowing the town down with their literature, he will remain completely aloof from any preaching on the subject. He may have friends on both sides, consider "that there are good points on both sides," and "not want to do anything that would interfere with his preaching the Gospel," so he takes no part in the controversy. The elders and he may agree to let others take all of the responsibility for meeting the hobbyists' attacks on the truth of this matter and keep their congregation free of all controversy. Such preachers and elders as those of this type would allow the church to be taken over by false teachers. In private, they will applaud your efforts to save the church and protect the untaught from confusion and error, but they will do nothing in public. In the book of Obadiah, God condemned Edom for being "on the other side" when enemy nations plundered his brother Judah. Edom did nothing against Judah, but did not lift his hand to help him in the struggle against pagan nations. Preachers and elders who give no assistance in opposing error in life or doctrine, but evade any position in a controversy which will inflame evil men against them, are exactly the same in principle as Edom, condemned

of God in this book. Then, when the battle is won, these say-nothing preachers and elders who stay out of any fight will reap the benefits, proclaim their soundness and even criticize those whose opposition to error made possible the security of their position. Here is the sure mark of the opportunist, and he is far more dangerous than the out-and-out false teacher, for if the tide of battle goes against truth and in favor of error, then he will emerge as friendly with error and still standing for nothing! Truly he is "a reed shaken with the wind." (Matt. 11:7)

2. He preaches what people of leadership or money want, regardless of principles.
3. He proceeds exactly as politicians bidding for national support in an election, stressing those points desired by the public where he is making a major address, and avoiding points that are needed, but which are unpopular with that section. For instance, a preacher may be known as positive in his pulpit condemnation of adultery, but he comes to a congregation for a meeting where the elders and preacher say little or nothing against it, and where those who want to live in adultery attend services "with comfort"—and there he says nothing against adultery! He calls that being "as wise as a serpent and as harmless as a dove." Actually, he is harming the church, in using his influence to cover and endorse a sin that will bar heaven to people. Still another preacher makes a clear distinction between the church and denominationalism where a church wants that stressed, but says practically nothing of it where the leading influences are opposed to such preaching. And another one will particularize points of worldliness, such as drinking, gambling, and dancing, in some places, but never mention them elsewhere.
4. One sure mark of an opportunist is that he generalizes instead of being specific. Mark this down, young men: Satan never objects to your preaching against sin, as long as you make your preaching general. But, when you become specific, and name what is sin, then is when the howl is raised. Certainly we agree that a preacher can go off half-cocked, decide that

something is worldly, and brand that practice without any basis in fact or without benefit of New Testament proof. Be sure, therefore, that what you believe to be worldly has been tested by its nature and history to establish that it is worldly. That is why I level my guns so much at dancing, drinking, gambling, and profanity. I could preach against worldliness and sin from now on and never arouse any opposition if I would stop right there. But when I specify those acts which are worldly, then is when Satan rears his ugly head. And the opportunist is smart enough to see that, and he never or rarely gets down to the "brass tacks" of being specific.

D. A preacher is a public man, has a public trust, and is open for public inspection. There are reasons for that.
   1. He claims to preach the truth.
   2. "The truth shall make you free." (John 8:32) That establishes the supreme importance of the truth.
   3. The people have a right, therefore, to know what is the truth. To hold back from people what is the truth is to deny to people that which will guide their soul to eternal heaven and away from eternal hell.
   4. The preacher has a position, an influence. He enjoys public confidence. People look to him for guidance. They have a right to know where he stands on any point. He should not content himself with saying, "If they want to know where I stand, let them ask me." That smacks of publicizing a stand on a controversial question as little as possible, rather than having the courage to volunteer information so as to place one's influence squarely where it belongs. That means that one is thinking more about calls for meetings and residence work than of the need for influencing people for the right. There is too much of this going on among our people. Brethren sometimes say that this is being level-headed, whereas it actually is fear to make a stand known lest doors be closed to calls. The best of men can be guilty if they are not careful. It is so easy to follow the path of least resistance. No, I am not advocating unnecessary agitation or riding a hobby to the hurt of the church. These lectures elsewhere have warned against such obnoxious action. But here we urge more courage, less opportunism,

and the fact that the brotherhood should know where a preacher stands on a question.

E. Yet, it is proper to temper conviction with judgment as to procedure, even in matters of doctrine. It is true that sometimes people cannot bear a certain point and are too inflamed to listen to you on a given subject. I am not denying that. That is a principle of action which we must all study. The application must be made with all of the wisdom of which we are capable. There is such a thing as a man being right and wrong at the same time: right in position, but wrong in procedure. So, let nothing said here against opportunism be construed as favorable to the unwise rubbing of salt into a wound beyond the ability of people to endure. But the danger here is this: that we may allow such a fact to be a pretext to justify evasion. I shudder at the danger of saying one thing to encourage any preacher to become a menace to the church by being senseless in his ardor in "taking a stand"; but I shudder just as much at the thought of encouraging one to evade issues and take stands in proportion as such actions influence popularity over the brotherhood.

F. Finally, if taking a stand on an issue gets you fired from a job, you have these five compensations:
   1. You have obeyed your Lord, and that is always right. There is no substitute for doing right. Nor should there be any apology for it.
   2. You have our Lord's assurance that such a sacrifice will have adequate compensation in the future life. "For whosoever would save his life shall lose it; and whosoever shall lose his life for my sake and the Gospel's shall save it." (Mark 8:35) We preach much to the world that "we walk by faith." (2 Cor. 5:7) Suppose we try practicing what we preach.
   3. You will have your self-respect. Isn't that worth much? There are popular preachers who have seared their consciences and may not now even be aware that they have lost that self-respect.
   4. Ordinarily, the right type of churches will hear that you were fired for standing for the right, and they will turn to you as the kind of preacher which they want. You will have the best sort of work, after all. That means, then, that there will also be compensa-

tion in this life.
5. You will come nearer being worth something in your influence to those souls who want to stand for the right. You will strengthen them, and eternity alone will reveal just how much help you have been to those who needed strengthening. It is worth much to know that we have helped others to be strong, instead of helping to tear down their resistance by spineless opportunism.

But, regardless of the results in this life of your stand on any question, the only kind of preaching that is not cowardly and selfish, that will please our God and save mankind, is that which takes a stand on the right, and then stands there, regardless of what happens to the preacher in this life. With all of the sincerity and interest of my heart, young brethren, I beg of you this: settle this point before you do any more preaching.

II. Discouragement.

A. I have reserved for the last major topic to leave with you that which is probably the Gospel preacher's number one enemy—discouragement. This, probably more than any other cause, influences more preachers to abandon right and adopt opportunism, lose their effectiveness, or entirely abandon the pulpit. If you are by nature inclined to be discouraged, this place in your make-up needs special attention. If you are stronger in this part of your character than the average person, you will need to major on strengthening this point. Scriptural proof for that is seen in the example of the apostle Paul. He was distinguished for his fighting. He stressed the word bold in his writings and preaching. (1 Thess. 2:2) He stood against opposition, without and within the church, with a firmness, sacrifice, and endurance which was at once both inspiring and almost unbelievable. (2 Cor. 11:23-28) Discouragement seemed to be no part of his character. However, he acknowledged his need for personal discipline. (1 Cor. 9:27) Further, upon one occasion of conflict and persecution, the Lord intervened to give Paul encouragement, in order to strengthen him for the emergency. The strongest man is made not so much of steel as to be without need for protection against discouragement.

B. In combatting discouragement, here are some abiding and practical points to guide you.
   1. First, on any given issue, make sure that you are right. Examine and re-examine, study and re-study. Think before you open your mouth and commit yourself. First making sure that you are taking a correct position will give point to your later action.
   2. Then, stand there without flinching, "...and having done all, to stand." (Eph. 6:13) All that the New Testament teaches on the subjects of love, kindness, gentleness, forbearance, patience, consideration for others, and kindred subjects, will not cancel or lessen the New Testament order for a Gospel preacher to stand, with unyielding firmness, in the face of any discouragement.
   3. Do NOT worry about the outcome, even if taking a correct position causes you to lose your job.
      a. If you have to leave because you are right, you will gain in the long run, both in this life and in the eternity to come. Proof: "Jesus said, 'Verily I say unto you, There is no man that hath left house, or brethren, or sisters, or mother, or father, or children, or lands, for My sake, and for the Gospel's sake, but he shall receive a hundredfold now in this time, houses, and brethren, and sisters, and mothers, and children, and lands, with persecutions; and in the world to come eternal life.'" (Mark 10:29-30) Either you believe that or you do not. If you do not, you should stop preaching. If you do, then use it frequently to add to your faith and increase your courage.
      b. But if you take a correct position in the face of dangerous opposition, and you do not have to leave, you still have gained. You have strengthened the position of the truth and the faith of those whom you teach and influence, as well as yourself.
      c. So, to take a right position and stand there, without worrying over the outcome, will make you win in either event. This is one place where you just cannot lose.
   4. Don't grow bitter if you do not receive proper credit from the very place where you should receive the

most. You will find this point to be especially important later on in your preaching life, unless you decide to just go along and follow the path of least resistance, never making any special stand against anything.
   a. You will find this caution especially appropriate if some day you accept a job with a church which has had severe internal trouble, making a harmful spectacle of itself, and you help that church to restore order out of chaos. Most preachers steer clear of such places, and I certainly do not recommend much dealing with congregations of that sort. But you may occasionally find yourself in the position of seeing a real challenge in such a problem. It may be placed before you in such a way that you see a great opportunity to help the cause of Christ there. You even feel a profound sense of duty, especially if others have detoured and fled the task. You may take the job, help to lead the church out of the wilderness of confusion and disgrace—even to the point of helping to mend an eldership which had become helpless, listen to the praises of those who loudly proclaim the earthly guidance and strength you supplied, be with the church in a period of reconstruction, solidification, and happiness—and then find the very ones most helped by you showing the least appreciation. That may never happen. It could. If it does, I repeat: school yourself not to grow bitter.
   b. Sometimes others will reap the benefits that you made possible. You may go through that hard period and supply the leadership which leads to better days, both spiritually and materially. After you leave, others will be quick to rush in and preach for such a place. They looked the other way when the church cried for a preacher in an emergency. But once everything runs smoothly and the church is out of danger, on the upward grade, it is no trouble for them to obtain preachers. Such a man will come in, knowing little of the inside problems, and may be critical of the very procedures you used to make his work possible. But he enjoys the blessings you helped to make

possible.
   c. But you still have received great—and sufficient—reward. If you are disappointed at times, serving spineless and ungrateful men, you can look back on a job of which you can be justifiably proud, and you can look to heavenly rewards. You have the satisfaction of knowing what happened. And the Lord knows. With all of my heart, young brethren, I believe and insist that this is enough reward, enough to keep you from growing bitter, enough to make you glad that you accepted that challenge and without regrets.
5. Don't grow bitter if other men receive more public recognition. Be extremely careful not to be tainted by the spirit of envy of other preachers. Some very "big names" give every sign of being envious of each other, of the praise that others receive, and of the way they are in demand over the brotherhood. There is plenty of work for everyone, and sufficient credit, both here and hereafter. Besides, is human credit that for which we are striving? I agree that it helps. The man is too cold who is not helped by human encouragement. In fact, such a character does not exist. It helps any of us. But take care lest we depend upon it too much, lest we cannot get along without it, lest we reach the place where it is an aim. Right here it would be profitable to do much reading and study of Matt. 6:1-8.
6. Finally, in these pointers on combatting discouragement, let us not be overwhelmed or bitter when we are "double-crossed" by someone. There will always be "disciples of the cross and double-cross." You will always find people in the church who will encourage you to take a stand on an issue, who will talk with vigor in private, but who will not stand with you in public or to others. One of the chief weaknesses of preachers—myself included—is this: we will see something which desperately needs to be done; no one else will do it; the church of the Lord will suffer if it is not done; we will then wade into it and attend to the dirty work. Then, the very ones in the church who agreed with us privately that the job should be done and who said, "Go to it; you can do it," will be

the first ones to be silent when you need support from critics over that very problem. If there is a weak leadership in a church, perhaps a divided eldership (and that surely is a weak leadership), many people will turn to you to see that needed tasks are handled—but some of them will be the first ones to turn against you when it is to their personal and selfish advantage. I have known of many such cases. One lesson to be learned is to go slow in attending to other people's dirty work for them. Tell them to do their own talking. But even then, there will be times when you will be so interested in and anxious for the progress of Christ's church that you will feel that you just have to go after a problem and see that it is solved, even though you know that the people most benefitted will later turn against you. The church would be much better off without the services or membership of every preacher, elder, and other member who wants you to take the knocks, and who will not stand up publicly before the church and in conversation with chronic and fickle critics and put them in their place, regardless of how meek and pious and sweet a front they put on. They are among the worst enemies of the church. But we will always have them, so understand that, do not allow that to discourage you or deter you from doing what you know is right. You and God will know who is responsible for the church's success. And, though credit and encouragement from men go a long way in helping a Christian, they are not by any means the most important things of life. Remember this: if you are abused by "a doubleminded man, unstable in all his ways" (James 1:8), God will stand. So will Christ. So will many Christians of whom you may not be aware. "If God is for us, who is against us?" (Rom. 8:31)

C. You are doing the greatest work of any set of men on earth, and you cannot afford to allow Satan to knock you out by using this most powerful weapon that he has. There is no place in the pulpit for the sissy. That work calls for fortitude. We of the churches of Christ do considerable preaching on "walking by faith." (2 Cor. 5:7) Then, let us practice what we preach. "I will in no wise fail thee, neither will I in any wise forsake thee." (Heb.

13:5) Do we believe that? If the prospect of hardship calls out any timidity in you, then try to fill your heart with the spirit of these Scriptures. In the face of any discouragement, begin to think on Scriptures of that sentiment. And combine that thinking with overflowing measures of prayer. There is no substitute for prayer, neither is there any Christianity without it. The best of preachers will make serious mistakes of judgment. But do not allow those mistakes or the false actions of others to cause you to fall under the heavy hand of discouragement. "I can do all things in Him that strengtheneth me." (Phil. 4:13) In this course of lectures, we have listed and considered a multitude of responsibilities and problems of the Gospel preacher, especially as he majors in working full time with a congregation. But do not be either dismayed or discouraged by either the wide scope or the severity of those burdens. There will always be the guarantee of help from the Lord and righteous disciples. And, if there can be found help from no disciple, the help from God will be sufficient. "My grace is sufficient for thee." (2 Cor. 12:9) The compensations far outweigh the sacrifices. If we suffer in time, we are building for eternity.

D. May God bless you and all Gospel preachers in your work of preaching the pure Gospel of Christ. May He bless your families. If they encourage you, you are wonderfully blessed. If they withhold that encouragement and only extend criticism, may He give them time to repent and add to your effectiveness by holding up your hands in this labor of love in proclaiming the Gospel of Christ. May He sustain you in every problem and crisis, of which there will be many, leading you out of the valley of mistakes and clouds to the high ground of achievement and light. May you become more and more effective in converting people and developing congregations, "looking unto Jesus the Author and Perfector of our faith, who for the joy that was set before Him endured the cross, despising shame, and hath sat down at the right hand of the throne of God." (Heb. 12:2).